For Reference

Not to be taken from this room

Revised, updated, expanded

Read to me ...
And I'll read to you

Reading Involvement
With Your Child From Birth

For Reference

Not to be taken from this room

BARBARA A. KOHLI
CAROLYN N. TROUTWINE

LIBRARY · HOME · SCHOOL · BOOKS

THE CLEARY CONNECTION, INC.
Arcanum, Ohio

FOR OUR CHILDREN

Publisher's Cataloging in Publication
(Prepared by Quality Books Inc.)

Kohli, Barbara Ann.
    Read to me—and I'll read to you: reading involvement with your child from birth /
Barbara A. Kohli, Carolyn N. Troutwine. — Rev., updated and expanded ed.
    p. cm.
    Includes bibliographical references.
    Preassigned LCCN: 94-94488.
    ISBN 0-9624195-1-6
    1. Reading (Early childhood)—United States. 2. Reading (Primary)—United States. 3.
Reading—United States—Parent participation. 4. Children—United States—Books and
reading. 5. Children's literature—Bibliography. I. Troutwine, Carolyn N. II. Title

LB1050.2.K64 1994   372.4'1
                                          QBI94-1421

ISBN 0-9624195-1-6

The Cleary Connection, Inc.
P.O. Box 310
Arcanum, Ohio 45304

Manufactured in the United States of America

Contents

Read to me ...
And I'll read to you

ACKNOWLEDGMENTS

My earliest memories are of my sister bringing piles of books home from school and the library to read each evening. And she's still reading — books always close by. She is a tremendous source of information, has an extensive vocabulary, and captivates the listener with descriptive, colorful language when she speaks. I have seen the difference books made in my sister's life and this example has been the driving force behind my efforts to get the best books to children for "their feast." Thank you, Marilyn.

Carolyn

The task of gathering books for review was made possible by the very efficient staff at the Northmont Branch of the Dayton and Montgomery County Public Library. Thank you! We are grateful to Stephen Richmond and Jennie Eisnaugle for their support.

Endless examination of the newest and finest titles for children was kindly offered at Books & Company in Dayton, Ohio where we received valuable assistance from Donna Gillis. Thank you!

Lastly, to the children, our own and those in our classrooms, who giggled, laughed out loud, cheered, sniffled and "oohed and aahed," thank you for showing the way to those wonderful child-pleasing books. We dedicate this book to you. Happy reading, good lives!

FOREWORD

As parents, educators and knowledgeable citizens, we are in touch with (and touched by) the many problems and challenges impacting education now. Our fundamental concerns must be with the welfare of children and their preparation for coping with this complex and constantly changing world. More than ever before, the processes and skills of problem solving, reasoning and sound decision making need to be taught and practiced. In overcrowded classrooms with culturally diverse populations and evolving curricula, we look to our schools to initiate programs that will connect classroom and home with activities that will help children succeed academically.

Supplementing and supporting at home what happens during the school day is receiving public attention, prompted by books detailing what a child in each primary grade should know or sets of cards with general information questions by grade level being easily and widely available. Using ready-made materials, though, is only a small part of addressing the problem of adequate instruction. Parent involvement with children on a daily basis beyond just asking, "What happened at school today?" is becoming a crucial need. Guiding, explaining, demonstrating, directing, challenging children through each day ultimately sparks curiosity and provides invaluable experiences. Selective TV viewing (TV off when not watching), and reading aloud with discussion and conversation are major interventions that make positive differences in children's lives.

We hear so much about spending quality time with our kids. The ultimate quality time can be shared reading experiences with outstanding books as the medium for enjoyable and rewarding communication. My sons and daughter, now in their thirties, remember practicing their letters from *Curious George Learns the Alphabet* or looking forward to a new installment of *The Wonderful Adventures of Nils.* Many of their happiest memories are anchored to what they were reading at any point in development, or what was read to them. Early experiences with books (particularly at home) countered and balanced later exposure to media influences like TV, and contributed toward making them, as they are today, enthusiastic lifetime readers.

In the 25 years that I worked as a school librarian and secondary language arts teacher, I was constantly engaged in locating and presenting the finest examples of literary genres for use in the classroom. A regret that I now have, looking back, is that I sometimes felt guilty when reading aloud to my students, as though that was not direct instruction or a really acceptable use of our time together. Comments from former students, though, consistently have emphasized their enjoyment of literature read aloud and class discussion of the "good parts" and reinforced my belief that we *can* make a difference if we carefully select the finest books for our children.

I can remember with so much pride the evaluations that came home with my kids as they progressed through school. Sharing current events, discussing books and articles we had read and analyzing issues were all derived from early experiences that bonded us to reading and each other. I felt like an important person and significant resource successful in passing along varied values and attitudes — to my own children and those in my junior high classes. In spending regular practice time with your children, reading and discussing what you have read, you can have that wonderful feeling too!

Lindy Hall
Boulder, Colorado

INTRODUCTION

Our children are growing up in a world far different than that of their grandparents. In general, theirs was a simpler life with fewer choices and a slower pace. They found entertainment where they were — in neighborhood ball games, stories on the radio, or comic books and nickel novels. Our world today offers children a dazzling array of diversions — in their toys, their games, in the channels available on the television dial. It is a world of fast food, flashy entertainment, and aggressive marketing of products from toothpaste to snacks. Children are offered a daily range of organized activities from art and music lessons to dance instruction to a variety of athletic opportunities featuring individual and team sports. Often, it seems that few moments can be salvaged for creative play or the quietly-active pastime of reading. It is during play that young minds are imagining, inventing, problem solving and role playing. It is while reading (or listening to someone else read) that children can contemplate, analyze, categorize or just plain relax. It is not difficult to see how, with our busy lives, these vital activities can get lost in the shuffle.

We believe that if our children are to discover the joy of reading, we, the adults, are going to have to bring experiences to them. To this end, we have painstakingly scoured the thousands upon thousands of currently available children's books to find those most likely to help you succeed in bringing this gift to your children.

Barbara Kohli, educator, parent and co-creator of this project, has detailed a progression of books for children (spanning stages infant through school age) that grew as a result of her own attempts to quickly locate books that were age and interest appropriate for her own boys. This progression, while not limiting selection, allows for unique differences in development yet recognizes the fact that most children do follow a series of fairly predictable stages in the enjoyment of books.

The following categories give parents tried-and-true assistance in what can often be a confusing, even overwhelming task of finding books for their youngsters.

- Parent/Child Involvement Books. . .finger plays, rhymes, and songs
- Point and Name Books. . . .. board books with bright colored single objects
- Talk-Abouts. . . .. pictures of common objects and everyday routines as well as illustrations that encourage conversation
- Describe-A-Page .... one or two sentences describing what is in the picture
- Stories with Simple Plot. . ... pictures and one or two lines of story

- Books with Plot. . ... defined plot with beginning, middle and end
- Chapter Books. . . .. longer stories

We invite you to accompany us through the following pages as we share what we have learned in the course of years in the classroom and countless experiences in reviewing and enjoying thousands of children's books.

Barbara Kohli
Carolyn Troutwine

WHY DO WE READ?

ENTERTAINMENT — Children love to hear a good story! It's just fun! But they don't realize that their minds are active, their imaginations are growing and their vocabularies are expanding.

ENRICHMENT — Books fill their sights with wonderful works of art in a glorious array of colors, media, and styles. They fill their minds with words lovely in their sounds and motions. Nowhere else can children hear the beauty of their native language in its written form.

EXPERIENCES — Books take them to the Swiss Alps or a deserted tropical island or a cave in ancient North America. Reading introduces them to Captain Hook, Madame Curie, or Michael Jordan. There is a world of places and people to be discovered in books.

ESCAPE — Maybe your child just had an argument with a best friend, or is afraid of a thunderstorm, or is in a bad mood. What better way to whisk him or her away from problems for awhile than by reading a good book.

EMOTIONAL BONDS — Something truly special happens between reader and listener. It is a time between adult and child that is free from stress and expectations. There is warmth and closeness that lasts for years to come.

KNOWLEDGE — Children soak up interesting facts and information like sponges. From giant dinosaurs to microscopic parasites, from bridges to pyramids, from sunspots to earthquakes and from papermaking to Native American crafts - it's all found in books.

EMPATHY AND SENSITIVITY — In a well-written book, the author draws the reader into the lives of characters; their thoughts, insecurities, strengths, and weaknesses. The skilled use of words evokes sympathy and understanding. What a wonderful way to promote empathy for people different from ourselves!

IMPROVED MENTAL ABILITIES — From the pages of books come descriptions of places, events, characters and ideas. This material enters your brain. Then your mental processes go to work. You form mental pictures of what you've read. You can pause, reflect back over the story or predict what will happen next. You remember information you learned in the past and make connections with the new information. The more bits of information you know, the more connections you are capable of, the more meaningful the information becomes. In other words, the more you read and take in, the easier it is to understand new material.

AUTHORS' NOTE

Great care was taken in selecting the books for our list. We strove to select books excellent in artistic and literary quality and equally important, ones which tugged at our emotions. It is, by no means, all-inclusive but it is a starting point. The levels are also starting points — children will enjoy books from several levels once they are experienced listeners and are hooked on books. A six-year old may want to hear *The Chronicles of Narnia* one night and *Goodnight Moon* the next. A child just beginning to listen may need to start in a level lower than his chronological age. (You will find the author and illustrator(s) on the first lines and the title below.)

It is very important that adults read the books they have selected before reading aloud, for appropriateness of language and support of their values. Children also vary greatly in sensitivity - what is too emotionally mature for one is perfect for another.

Barbara and Carolyn

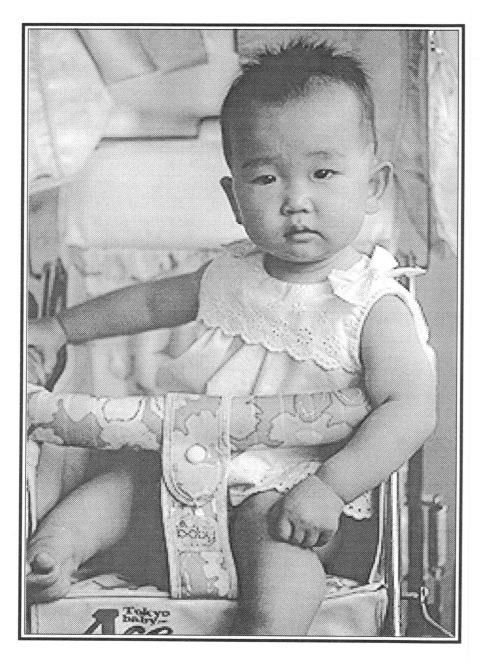

Infant

Infant

OBSERVING THE INFANT

Newborn infants spend the first few weeks of their lives sleeping, eating and slowly becoming aware of the world around them. At first, they communicate with us by crying when they are hungry or uncomfortable. They try to turn their heads toward our voices — first with a little wobble from side to side, then with a definite focus on our faces. Later, they cuddle when held, smile at friendly faces, coo with pleasure, and wave  their arms and legs when excited. By the time their first birthdays roll around they babble and may even say a few words. They may raise their arms to get their mother's attention, frown when tasting something unpleasant and laugh when amused.

WHAT PARENTS CAN DO

As parents, we are well aware of our roles as caregivers — feeding, bathing, clothing and diapering, and as nurturers — cuddling, comforting and loving. But we also find we are entertainers. We talk and sing, we bounce and kiss, we wind up lullaby mobiles and strategically place mirrors and brightly-colored objects as we try to catch our infant's gaze. We gently tickle little tummies, make silly faces, nibble tiny fingers and toes, all with the hope of capturing those baby smiles and giggles. These gentle exchanges between parent and child form the bonds of communication that set the stage for later thought processes and language skills.

THE INFANT AND BOOKS

During this first year, books can be a natural and easy part of our babies' entertainment. First, books can provide the material for baby's first contact with language spoken in a way different from our normal conversation. The rhythms and sing-songy pattern of nursery rhymes and jingles seem to delight many babies, especially when used with bouncing games and finger and toe plays. The soothing flow of lulla-bies, whether sung or spoken softly may calm a fretful baby. Second, books provide visual interest for even the newest babies. They like, for a few seconds at least, to look at bold patterns — especially sharp contrasts such as black against white or large, simple, colorful pic-tures of faces, animals or objects.

Some babies will lie quietly while a book is being read. Perhaps they are lulled by the comfortable sound of the reading voice along with the pleasure of cuddling. Try it with your baby. If successful, great, you've made a wonderful start toward connecting reading with pleasure. Is your baby too active or won't tolerate reading. Don't worry, there's plenty of time later when your baby is ready.

As the little ones approach their first birthdays, they will enjoy, more and more, books with pictures of familiar things. An important mile-stone for a baby is realizing that the duck in the picture book is the same as the duck in the park pond, that the picture of the ball is the same as a real ball, and so on. Parents can encourage this understand-ing by pointing to and naming the objects on each page, especially the more familiar ones. Many babies will want to have this activity re-peated over and over again. With all this repetition and enjoyment, they are well on their way to making sense of the world around them. At the same time, the closeness and warmth of parent and child helps to form emotional bonds with books. Already, your baby has begun to form a lifelong love of reading.

TIPS FOR PARENTS OF INFANTS

1. If your baby wants to grab the book you're reading, try offering him one of his own to hold.

2. To get the baby's attention, first read a familiar book before trying new ones.

3. Continue to expose your infant to books even if you don't get a spectacular reaction.

4. Always carry books — great for soothing and breaks the monotony of baby's day.

Infant Booklist

Atkinson, Allen
Mother Goose's Nursery Rhymes
Bernal, Richard
Night Zoo
Blegvad, Lenore/Blegvad, Erik
This Is Me
Bradman, Tony & Williams, Jenny
This Little Baby
Bruna, Dick
Animal Book
Burningham, John
Cluck Baa
Cousins, Lucy
Country Animals
Cousins, Lucy
Farm Animals
Cousins, Lucy
Garden Animals
Cousins, Lucy
Pet Animals
Cuddle Books
What Do Babies Do
dePaola, Tomie
Baby's First Christmas
Evans, Michael
Wheels
Foord, Jo
The Book of Babies
Foord, Jo (photographed by)
The Book Of Babies
Good, Mike and Shott, Steve (Photographs by)
All About Baby
Good, Mike and Shott, Steve (Photographs by)
Baby and Friends
Good, Mike and Shott, Steve (Photographs by)

Good Morning, Baby
Good, Mike and Shott, Steve (Photographs by)
Good, Night, Baby!
Greeley, Valerie
Animals At Home
Greeley, Valerie
Field Animals
Greeley, Valerie
Zoo Animals
Hoban, Tana
Black On White
Hoban, Tana
White On Black
Hutchins, Pat
Where's the Baby?
Inkpen, Mick
Anything Cuddly Will Do!
Inkpen, Mick
This Troll, That Troll
Johnson, B. J.
BAA BAA Book
Johnson, Audean
Soft As A Kitten
Johnson, B. J.
Wheels
Kightley, Rosalina
ABC

Leslie, Amanda
Play Puppy Play
Lincoln, Frances (text)/Riddell, Edwina
100 First Words to Say With Your Baby
Lincoln, Frances (concepts)/Sieveking, Anthea (photographs)
What's Inside
Lionni, Leo
Let's Play
Lynn, Sara
Food
Lynn, Sara
Garden Animals
Lynn, Sara
Home
Lynn, Sara
Toys
Miller, Margaret
At My House
Miller, Margaret
In My Room
Miller, Margaret
Me and My Clothes
Miller, Margaret
More First Words - On My Street
Miller, Margaret
My First Words - Time to Eat
Moore, Dessie and Chevelle
Getting Dressed
Moore, Dessie and Chevelle
Good Morning
Moore, Dessie and Chevelle
Good Night
Moore, Dessie and Chevelle
Let's Pretend
Morgan, Jane Conteh
Colors
Morris, Ann/Roffey, Maureen
Animals
Morris, Ann/Roffey, Maureen
Clothes
Morris, Ann/Roffey, Maureen
Home

Morris, Ann/Roffey, Maureen
Toys
Ormerod, Jan
The Saucepan Game
Paterson, Bettina
Baby's ABC
Paterson, Bettina
In My House
Paterson, Bettina
In My Yard
Paterson, Bettina
My Clothes
Paterson, Bettina
My First Animals
Paterson, Bettina
My First Wild Animals
Paterson, Bettina
My Toys
Patrick, Denise Lewis/Cruickshank, Kathy
What Does Baby Hear?
Platt & Munk (pub.)/Seiden, Art
Trucks
Ricklen, Neil
Baby's Clothes
Ricklen, Neil
Baby's Colors
Ricklen, Neil
Baby's Friends
Ricklen, Neil
Baby's Home
Ricklen, Neil
Baby's Toys
Ricklen, Neil
Daddy and Me
Ricklen, Neil
Grandma and Me
Ricklen, Neil
Grandpa and Me
Ricklen, Neil
Mommy and Me
Salt, Jane/Hawksley
First Words For Babies and Toddlers
Shone, Venice

My Activity Box
Shone, Venice
My Lunch Box
Shone, Venice
My Play Box
Shone, Venice
My Toy Box
Sieveking, Anthea (photographs by)/
Lincoln, Frances (concepts)
What's Inside?
Slien, Debby
Baby's Words
Slien, Debby
Hello Baby
Steptoe, John
Baby Says
Tafuri, Nancy
In A Red House
Tafuri, Nancy
My Friends
Tafuri, Nancy
Two New Sneakers
Tafuri, Nancy
Where We Sleep
Tallarico, Tony
Here We Go
Tallarico, Tony
Who Am I
Teddy Board Books, Platt & Munk
(pub.)
Baby's First Book
Teddy Board Books, Platt & Munk
(pub.)
Baby's Seasons
Teddy Board Books, Platt & Munk
(pub.)
Baby's Things
Tucker, Sian
My Toys
Tucker, Sian
Noises
Tucker, Sian
Sizes
Van Fleet, Matthew
One Yellow Lion

Ziefert, Harriet/Gorbaty, Norman
Baby Ben's Busy Book
Ziefert, Harriet/Gorbaty, Norman
Baby Ben's Go-Go Book

BOOKS FOR PARENTS TO USE AS RESOURCE

The following are books for parents to use. They are sources of rhymes, jingles, lullabies or fingerplays and bouncing games. They probably do not have pictures that babies are interested in, but keep them, because toddlers and pre-schoolers may enjoy them.

Brown, Marc
Finger Rhymes
Brown, Marc
Hand Rhymes
Brown, Marc
Play Rhymes
Chorao, Kay
The Baby's Bedtime Book
Chorao, Kay
The Baby's Lap Book
Craig, Helen
I See The Moon, and The Moon Sees Me. . .
de Angeli's, Marguerite
Book of Nursery and Mother Goose Rhymes
De Regaiers, Beatrice Schenk; More, Eva; White, Mary; Carr, Jan
Sing A Song of Popcorn Every Child's Book of Poems
Edens, Cooper (selected by)
The Glorious Mother Goose
Emerson, Sally (selected by)/Maclean, Moira and Colin
The Nursery Treasury - A collection of Baby Games, Rhymes, and Lullabies
Fox, Mem
Time For Bed

Grover, Eulalie, Osgood/Frederick
Richardson
**Mother Goose - The Classic
Volland Edition**
Hague, Kathleen/Michael Hague
**Out of the Nursery, Into the
Night**
Harness, Cheryl
The Night-Light Mother Goose
Jones, Carol (illustrated by)
**Hickory Dickory Dock and
Other Nursery Rhymes**
Meigs, Mildred Plew/Conover, Chris
Moon Song
Messenger, Jannat
Lullabies and Baby Songs
Opie, Iona and Peter
The Opie Rhyme Book
Opie, Iona and Peter
**Tail Feathers From Mother
Goose**
Oxenbury, Helen
**The Helen Oxenbury Nursery
Rhyme Book**
Piper, Watty (edited)/Tim and Greg
Hildebrandt
**A Treasury of Best Loved
Rhymes**
Plotz, Helen (compiled & edited)/
Marisabina, Russo
A Week of Lullabies
Prelutsky, Jack/Brown, Marc
Read-Aloud Rhymes
Ra, Carol F. (compiled by)/Stock,
Catherine (pictures by)
**Trot Trot To Boston - Play
Rhymes for Baby**
Rackham, Arthur
**Mother Goose Nursery
Rhymes**
Souci, Daniel San
**The Mother Goose Book - A
Collection of Nursery Rhymes**
Watson, Clyde
Father Fox's Pennyrhymes

Watson, Wendy
**Wendy Watson's Mother
Goose**
Wilkes, Angela (selected by)
Animal Nursery Rhymes

Toddler

Toddler

OBSERVING THE TODDLER

The toddler years, from the first to the third birthdays, are a time of enormous mental and physical growth. Because toddlers are rapidly gaining the skills that allow them to walk, run and climb, they are much freer to explore their sections of the world. They are curious about everything and they try to learn about each object they come in contact with. By putting objects in their mouths, turning them over and over, and even throwing, dropping and banging them, they learn — what is soft or hard, smooth or rough, what bounces, floats, rolls or makes noise. Important people get names — mama and dada — as well as important objects — bottles, pacifiers or blankets. The list grows, slowly at first and then faster, and eventually includes phrases and sentences.

WHAT PARENTS CAN DO

Parents' roles at this age are exhausting but rewarding ones. It takes lots of energy along with tons of patience to deal with all this motion and curiosity. Yet your impact on the child's mental development and feelings of accomplishment can be enormous. While toddlers work at all this physical exploring and naming, parents can help by talking, talking, talking to the youngsters and by giving them reasonable freedom to explore. Moms and dads can name objects — kitty, tree, balloon - as well as describe the objects, "kitty is soft (purring, sleeping)" "the tree is rough (very tall, has many leaves)" "the balloon is round (light, yellow)." They can talk about things the youngster *sees,* "There goes a long, long train," *hears,* "Listen to the soft patter of the rain," *tastes,* "This lemon tastes sour," *feels,* "Your hands are sticky from the orange," and, *Smells,* "Smell the brownies baking in the oven?" Parents can talk about what they (the adults) are doing:

"I'm cutting this banana into little pieces, so it will be easier for you to eat."

"Let's wash your arms first, now your hands . . . now your tummy . . . next your feet . . ."

"It's raining outside. Let's see, what will we need? Your jacket, your boots and an umbrella."

Children vitally need to experience real people, places and things. The more they experience the world, the better they will come to understand it and eventually find their own place in it. For enriching your children's experiences of the real people, places and things in their world — books are the thing. For providing even wider experiences — of the lives of the pioneers or the life of the American Indians, the building of the pyramids or the space shuttle — books are the thing! Finding time each day to enjoy books together adds to your children's experiences, expands their vocabularies, helps increase their understanding of the world, and if that's not enough, it also provides a quiet, warm and secure time between parents and children.

TODDLERS AND BOOKS

Toddlers still enjoy books they grew to love in their infancies and will want to go back to those "old friends" often. They also love to see pictures of familiar objects. Start with those books which have only one or two objects on a page and work up to more complex pictures. Youngsters love to point to a picture and ask "what's that?" to have you name the object. These "Point-and-Name" books are great ways to start conversations. "Look, there's a picture of a necklace. Mommy is wearing a necklace too. Did you get a necklace for your birthday?" You can help your child make connections between the picture and the real objects.

Older toddlers enjoy books with full-page or two-page spreads of scenes in which there are many details and much activity. These "talk-about books," such as *Richard Scarry's Best Word Book Ever,* involve parent and child in lots of pointing-to and naming as well as more involved conversation about the variety of activities on the pages.

At some point, toddlers begin to enjoy books which tell stories. The very first ones simply have movement through time — morning to evening or summer to winter. *Jesse Bear What Will You Wear?* by Nancy White Carlstrom follows little bear's day as he dresses in the morning until bedtime. *Pumpkin, Pumpkin* by Jeanne Titherington follows the growth of a seed to harvest.

Later, when toddlers are able to follow a story from beginning to end, try books with very simple story lines such as *Blueberries for Sal* by Robert McCloskey or Dick Bruna's *Snuffy*.

The main rule of thumb is to choose books your toddler responds to - whether special interests such as trucks, animals or teddy bears or books which reinforce feelings of security such as *Goodnight Moon* or *The Runaway Bunny* both by Margaret Wise Brown or books with lots of rhythm and rhyme as in *Jamberry* by Bruce Degen.

TIPS FOR PARENTS OF TODDLERS

1. Get down on the floor, sit on the porch or by the bathtub — anytime, anywhere for reading.

2. Leaf through a new book quickly telling the story or oohing and aahing to spark interest. Even pose questions such as, "Do you see the little mouse?"

3. Toddlers may appear disinterested in a new book. Keep reading even when they move away. The book then becomes familiar for future readings.

4. Wean toddlers over to books with simple plots by telling the story in your own words while quickly turning the pages. On the next reading, read a line or two on each page. Eventually, when the youngster knows what's going to happen and is interested, you'll be able to read the whole story.

5. Toddlers may enjoy filling in words or lines of rhymes and jingles.

Toddler Booklist

Ahlberg, Janet & Allan
The Baby's Catalogue
Ahlberg, Janet & Allan
Peek-A-Boo!
Aker, Suzanne/Karlin, Bernie
What Comes In 2's, 3's, & 4's?
Allen, Jonathan
Up the Stairs, Down the Slide
Allen, Jonathan
Purple Sock, Pink Sock
Allen, Jonathan
One With A Bun
Alexander, Martha
Good Night, Lily
Alexander, Martha
Lilly and Willy
Aliki
Hush Little Baby
Amery, Heather/Cartwright, Stephen
The Farm Picture Book
Amery, Heather/Cartwright, Stephen
The Zoo Picture Book
Anello,Christine/Thompson, Sharon
The Farmyard Cat
Archambault, John/Rombola, John
Counting Sheep
Asch, Frank
Baby in the Box
Asch, Frank
Goodnight Horsey
Asch, Frank
Just Like Daddy
Asch, Frank
Moonbear's Books
Asch, Frank
Moonbear's Canoe
Asch, Frank
Moonbear's Friend
Asch, Frank

Moonbear
Aylesworth, Jim/Christelow, Eileen
The Completed Hickory Dickory Dock
Aylesworth, Jim/Young, Ruth
One Crow - A Counting Rhyme
Baer, Gene/Ehlert, Lois
Thump, Thump, Rat-a-Tat-Tat
Bang, Molly
Ten, Nine, Eight
Barton, Byron
Airplanes
Barton, Byron
Airport
Barton, Byron
Boats
Barton, Byron
I Want To Be An Astronaut
Barton, Byron
Machines At Work
Barton, Byron
Trains
Barton, Byron

Trucks
Beck, Ian
Five Little Ducks
Bentley, Nancy
Do This, Hands
Bentley, Nancy
Let's Go, Feet
Bentley, Nancy
Listen To This, Ears
Bentley, Nancy
What's On Top, Head
Blanchard, Arlene/Julian-Ottie,Vanessa
Sounds My Feet Make
Bond, Michael/Lobban, John
Paddington's ABC
Bond, Michael/Lobban, John
Paddington's Colors
Bond, Michael/Lobban, John
Paddington's Opposites
Bond, Michael/Lobban, John
Paddington's 123
Bond, Michael
Paddington At the Seashore
Bond, Michael
Paddington In The Kitchen
Bond, Michael
Paddington Goes Shopping
Bond, Michael
Paddington Takes A Bath
Brown, Margaret Wise/Hurd, Clement
Goodnight Moon
Brown, Marc
Party Rhymes
Brown, Marc
Play Rhymes
Brown, Ruth
If At First You Do Not See
Brown, Ruth
Our Cat Flossie
Browne, Anthony
Things I Like
Bryant, Donna/Breeze, Lynn
One Day At The Park
Burningham, John
Cluck Baa

Burningham, John
Jangle Twang
Burningham, John
Skip Trip
Burningham, John
Slam Bang
Burningham, John
Sniff Shout
Burningham, John
Wobble Pop
Butterworth, Nick/Inkpen, Mick
Just Like Jasper!
Butterworth, Nick
**Nick Butterworth's Book of
Nursery Rhymes**
Campbell, Rod
Dear Zoo
Cauley, Lorinda Bryan
Clap Your Hands
Carle, Eric
1, 2, 3 to the Zoo
Craig, Helen
**I See The Moon & The Moon
Sees Me**
Carlstrom, Nancy White/Degen, Bruce
**Jesse Bear, What Will You
Wear?**
Carlstrom, Nancy White/Ormai, Stella
The Moon Came Too
Carter, David A.
More Bugs in Boxes
Carter, Margaret/Wright, Carol
Go Away, William
Cartwright, Stephen and Zeff, Claudia
Find The Bird
Cartwright, Stephen and Zeff, Claudia
Find The Duck
Cartwright, Stephen and Zeff, Claudia
Find The Kitten
Cartwright, Stephen and Zeff, Claudia
Find The Piglet
Cartwright, Stephen and Zeff, Claudia
Find The Puppy
Cartwright, Stephen and Zeff, Claudia
Find The Teddy

28

My Bye-Bye Bottle Book
Gelbard, Jane and Polivy, Betse Bober/
Klonsky, Arthur (photographs)
My Sharing Book
Gerstein, Mordicai
William, Where Are You?
Gibbons, Gail
Playgrounds
Gibbons, Gail
Trains
Gibbons, Gail
Trucks
Ginsburg, Mirra/Tafuri, Nancy
Across The Stream
Ginsburg, Mirra/Tafuri, Nancy
Asleep, Asleep
Goennel, Heidi
If I Were a Penguin
Gold, Ethel (illustrated by)
**Things That Go - Ladybird
Picture Books**
Gomi, Taro
Toot!
Gomi, Taro
Where's The Fish?
Graham, Bob
The Red Woolen Blanket
Greenfield, Eloise/Gilchrist, Jan Spivey
Big Friend, Little Friend
Greenfield, Eloise/Gilchrist, Jan Spivey
My Doll, Keshia
Griest, Virginia/Wellington, Monica
In Between
Hartman, Gail/Weiss, Ellen
**For Strawberry Jam or
Fireflies**
Hawkins, Colin and Jacqui
Dip, Dip, Dip
Hawkins, Colin and Jacqui
One Finger, One Thumb
Hawkins, Colin and Jacqui
Oops-A-Daisy
Hawkins, Colin and Jacqui
Where's Bear?
Hellard, Susan

Time to Get Up
Henkes, Kevin
SHHHH
Hennessy, B. G./Watson, Wendy
**A,B,C,D, Tummy, Toes, Hands,
Knees**
Hennessly, B. G./McCue, Lisa (based
on the character by Don Freeman)
Corduroy's Christmas
Hines, Anna Grossnickle
Moompa, Toby, And Bomp
Hoban, Tana
Of Colors And Things
Hill, Eric
Good Morning, Baby Bear
Hill, Eric
Spot's Big Book of Words
Hill, Eric
Spot's First Birthday
Hill, Eric
Spot's First Christmas
Hill, Eric
Spot's First Easter
Hill, Eric
Spot's First Walk
Hill, Eric
Spot's Toy Box
Hill, Eric
Where's Spot?
Hines, Anna/Hines, Anna Grossnickle
Taste The Raindrops
Hoban, Tana
Look! Look! Look!
Hoban, Tana
Red, Blue, Yellow Shoe
Hoffman, Phyllis/Wilson, Sarah
We Play
Hooker, Yvonne/Michelini, Carlo A
One Green Frog
Hooker, Yvonne/Michelini, Carlo A.
Wheels Go Round
Howard, Jane/Cherry, Lynne
When I'm Sleepy
Hughes, Shirley
Bouncing

Lindgren, Barbro/Eriksson, Eva
  Sam's Teddybear
MacDonald, Amy/Roffey, Maureen
  Let's Make A Noise
MacKinnon, Debbie/Sieveking
  What Shape?
Magnus, Erica
  My Secret Place
Maris, Ron
  Are You There Bear?
Maris, Ron
  Better Move On Frog
Maris, Ron
  Hold Tight, Bear
Maris, Ron
  In My Garden
Maris, Ron
  Is Anyone Home
Maris, Ron
  My Book
Marisabina, Russo
  The Line-up Book
Marzollo, Jean/Jeffers, Susan
  Close Your Eyes
McCue, Lisa
  Bunnies Love
McCue, Lisa
  Ducklings Love
McMillan, Bruce
  **Becca Backward, Becca
  Frontward - A Book of Con-
  cept Pairs**
McMillan, Bruce
  Growing Colors
McNaught, Harry
  Trucks
Melmed, Laura Krauss/Sorensen, Henri
  I Love You As Much
Meryl, Debra/Kelley, True
  **Baby's Peek-A-Boo Album - A
  Lift-the-Flap Book**
Miller, Margaret
  At My House
Miller, Margaret
  Can You Guess?

Miller, Margaret
  In My Room
Miller, Margaret
  Me and My Clothes
Miller, Margaret
  Where Does It Go?
Newton, Laura/Rogers, Jacqueline
  William the Vehicle King
Ormerod, Jan
  101 Things To Do With A Baby
Ormerod, Jan
  Bend and Stretch
Ormerod, Jan
  Dad's Back
Ormerod, Jan
  Making Friends
Ormerod, Jan
  Messy Baby
Ormerod, Jan
  Mom's Home
Ormerod, Jan
  Reading
Ormerod, Jan
  Sleeping
Ormerod, Jan
  This Little Nose
Ormerod, Jan
  Yes
Oxenbury, Helen
  Family
Oxenbury, Helen
  Good Night, Good Morning
Oxenbury, Helen
  Grandma and Grandpa
Oxenbury, Helen
  Monkey See, Monkey Do
Oxenbury, Helen
  Mother's Helper
Oxenbury, Helen
  Our Dog
Oxenbury, Helen
  Shopping Trip
Parker, Mary Jessie/Dennis, Lynne
  City Storm
Pelham, David/Foreman, Michael

Worms Wiggle
Philip Lief Group, Inc., The/Dunn,
Phoebe & Lee, Vincent B.
Big & Little
Philip Lief Group, Inc., The/Dunn,
Phoebe & Lee, Vincent B.
How Many?
Philip Lief Group, Inc., The/Dunn,
Phoebe & Lee, Vincent B.
Whose Baby Are You?
Pocock, Rita
Annabelle and the Big Slide
Pomerantz, Charlotte/Tafuri, Nancy
Flap Your Wings and Try
Pragoff, Fiona
Alphabet
Pragoff, Fiona
Growing
Pragoff, Fiona
How Many?
Pragoff, Fiona
Opposites
Pragoff, Fiona
Shapes
Pragoff, Fiona
What Color?
Rice, Eve
Sam Who Never Forgets
Rius, Maria/Parramon, J. M. and Puig,
J. J.
Fire
Rius, Maria/Parramon, J. M. and Puig,
J. J.
Sight
Rius, Maria/Parramon, J. M. and Puig,
J. J.
Smell
Rius, Maria/Parramon, J. M. and Puig,
J. J.
Taste
Rius, Maria/Parramon, J. M. and Puig,
J. J.
Touch
Rockwell, Anne
At The Playground

Rockwell, Anne/Rockwell, Lizzy
Pots And Pans
Rockwell, Anne
Big Wheels
Rockwell, Anne
Bikes
Rockwell, Anne
Fire Engines
Rockwell, Anne
First Comes Spring
Rockwell, Anne
In Our House
Rockwell, Anne
On Our Vacation
Rockwell, Anne
Things That Go
Rockwell, Anne
Things To Play With
Rockwell, Anne
Trucks
Roddie, Shen/Cony, Frances
Hatch, Egg, Hatch!
Roffey, Maureen
Bathtime
Roffey, Maureen
Mealtime
Rogers, Paul and Emma
Robinson,Colin
What's Wrong, Tom?
Rogers, Paul/Corfield, Robin Bell
Somebody's Sleepy
Root, Betty/Langley, Jonathan
My First Dictionary
Rosen, Michael/Oxenbury, Helen
We're Going on a Bear Hunt
Ross, Katharine/Hirashima, Jean
The Little Quiet Book
Ross, Katharine/Hirashima, Jean
The Little Noisy Book
Runcie, Jill/Lorenz, Lee
Cock-A-Doodle-Doo
Ruschak, Lynette/Hansen, Biruta
Akerbergs
Who's Hiding?
Salt, Jane/Hawksley, Gerald

First Words For Babies And Toddlers
Salt, Jane/Hawksley, Gerald
First Words And Pictures
Sawicki, Norma Jean/Goffe, Toni
The Little Red House
Scarry, Richard
Richard Scarry's Best Word Book Ever
Schroeder, Binette
Tuffa and The Snow
Scott, Ann/Coalson, Glo
On Mother's Lap
Seiden, Art
Trucks
Seymour, Peter/Carter, David
What's in the Jungle?
Shapiro, Arnold L./Wellington, Monica
Who Says That?
Shiffman, Lena (illustrated by)
My First Book Of Words
Slier, Debby and Koken, Tom/Dwight, Laura (photographs by)
Hello School
Spier, Peter
Gobble, Growl, Grunt
Spier, Peter
Noah's Ark
Spier, Peter
Peter Spier's Christmas
Steptoe, John
Baby Says
Stickland, Paul
A Child's Book of Things
Stott, Dorothy
Too Much
Szekeres, Cyndy
Sammy's Special Day
Szekeres, Cyndy
Suppertime For Frieda Fuzzypaws
Tafuri, Nancy
The Ball Bounced
Tafuri, Nancy

Early Morning In The Barn
Tafuri, Nancy
Follow Me
Tafuri, Nancy
Have You Seen My Duckling?
Tafuri, Nancy
Rabbit's Morning
Tafuri, Nancy
Spots, Feathers, and Curly Tails
Taylor, Judy/Cartwright, Reg
My Cat
Taylor, Judy/Cartwright, Reg
My Dog
Thompson, Brian/Berridge, Celia
Viking First Picture Dictionary
Titherington, Jeanne
Baby's Boat
Turner, Gwenda
Shapes
Van Vorst, M./Tomes, Margot
A Norse Lullaby
Voake, Charlotte
First Things First — A Baby's Companion
Wahl, Robert/Ewers, Joe
Friend Dog
Watanabe, Shiego/Ohtomo, Yasuo
How Do I Put It On?
Watanaba, Shiego/Ohtomo, Yasuo
I Can Build A House!
Watanaba, Shiego/Ohtomo, Yasuo
I Can Take A Walk
Watanaba, Shiego/Ohtomo, Yasuo
What A Good Lunch
Wildsmith, Brian
Animal Games
Wildsmith, Brian
Animal Tricks
Williams, Vera B.
'More, More, More, ' Said the Baby: Three Love Stories
Winograd, Deborah
My Color Is Panda
Wolff, Ashley

A Year of Beasts
Wood, Jakki/Bonner, Rog
Moo Moo, Brown Cow
Wood, Audrey
Oh My Baby Bear!
Yektai, Niki/Ryan, Susannah
What's Silly?
Yoshi
Yoshi 1, 2, 3
Young, Ruth/Isadora, Rachel
Golden Bear
Young, Ed
Seven Blind Mice
Young, Ruth
My Baby-sitter
Young, Ruth
My Blanket
Young, Ruth
The New Baby
Ziefert, Harriet
Get Set! Go!
Ziefert, Harriet/Boon, Emilie
Mommy, Where Are You?
Ziefert, Harriet
Where's My Easter Egg?
Zion, Gene/Graham, Margaret Bloy
Harry The Dirty Dog

The following are books with simple story lines which wean the toddler from books with pictures to books with actual stories.

Biegvad, Erik
The Three Little Pigs
Brett, Jan
Goldilocks And The Three Bears
Bruna, Dick
Snuffy
Fox, Mem/Mullins, Patricia
Hattie and the Fox
Freeman, Don

A Pocket For Corduroy
Freeman, Don
Corduroy
Galdone, Paul
The Three Little Pigs
Galvani, Maureen/Littler, Angela
What Can You See?
Gay, Michel
Take Me For A Ride
Jacobs, Joseph/Cauley, Lorinda Bryan
The Three Little Pigs
Kelly, Holly
Geraldine's Blanket
Koci, Marta
Katie's Kitten
Krauss, Ruth/Johnson, Crockett
The Carrot Seed
Lowrey, Janette S.
The Poky Little Puppy
McCloskey, Robert
Blueberries For Sal
McCloskey, Robert
Make Way For Ducklings
Oxenbury, Helen
Tom and Pippo In the Snow
Oxenbury, Helen
Tom and Pippo Read A Story
Oxenbury, Helen
Tom and Pippo's Day
Peppe, Rodney
The Three Little Pigs
Titherington, Jeanne
Pumpkin, Pumpkin

Pre-School

Pre-School

OBSERVING THE PRESCHOOLER

From somewhere around the third birthday until they enter school, children are in a wonderful age of discovery. At times they seem to ask an endless stream of questions and, because many of the concepts they are forming are inaccurate or incomplete, their questions may seem to make little sense. But to the child, they are very important. By questioning and talking, they work to understand the world around them. They are able to hold conversations with others and often do so with amazing persistence.

Their attention spans are lengthening and their interest in books is strong. While they reach out to the world around them, they still want to know that the security of their important grown-ups is within easy reach.

WHAT PARENTS CAN DO

In some ways, parents' jobs are getting somewhat easier now because preschoolers are able to handle many jobs such as eating and getting dressed by themselves. In other ways though, parents' jobs get more demanding. It is often tempting to shut out all those questions, but by treating them thoughtfully and respectfully and trying to answer them in terms not too simple nor too complex, parents can keep the active preschooler's mind thinking and growing.

Preschoolers enjoy a wide variety of books; in no other age-level is there such an abundance of delightful picture books. When borrowing books at the library, a collection of 20 or 30 (or more) is not too many. Be prepared to read some favorites over and over.

PRESCHOOLERS AND BOOKS

Preschoolers continue to enjoy books from toddlerhood, but they can easily follow story lines and will especially enjoy them if they are about children their own ages. They are often quite interested in other children's activities and difficulties and love to "stick with" a story to see how the problems or situations are solved. Good ones to start with are Shirley Hughes's *Alfie Gets in First* and *Alfie Lends a Hand* or *Hazel's Amazing Mother* by Rosemary Wells.

The gentler fairy tales, especially those with lots of repetition, are favorites. *The Three Billy Goats Gruff* illustrated by Janet Stevens, *Goldilocks and the Three Bears* illustrated by Jan Brett or *The Pancake Boy* illustrated by Lorinda Bryan Cauley are some good choices.

Preschoolers love books with nature topics. Some especially nice ones include Jim Arnosky's *Deer at the Brook, Raccoons and Ripe Corn* and *Watching Foxes* or David Bellamy's *The Roadside* and *The Rock Pool.* The Eyewitness series of books has beautiful yet clear and simple photographs which invite much discussion. They are available on a great variety of subjects, are complex enough for preschoolers through adults, and can be used in a variety of ways to suit the age of the child.

TIPS FOR PARENTS OF PRESCHOOLERS

1.   Your child may have definite tastes. Read books you select as well as those your child picks.
2.   Go back to old favorites as well as ahead to more complex story lines.
3.   Be patient with interruptions, comments and questions. These are all signs that the youngster is involved with the story and is enjoying it.
4.   Once in a while, try books you may think are too "advanced." Your preschooler may surprise you with interest and understanding.

Pre-School/Kindergarten Booklist

Aardema, Verna
  Bringing the Rain to Kapiti Plain
Adler, David A./Cruz, Ray
  You Think It's Fun To Be A Clown!
Ahlberg, Janet and Allan
  Each Peach Pear Plum
Albert, Burton/Pinkney, Brian
  Where Does The Trail Lead
Alborough, Jez
  Where's My Teddy?
Alexander, Martha
  Out! Out! Out!
Aliki
  Overnight At Mary Bloom's
Aliki
  The Two Of Them
Allard, Harry/Marshall, James
  I Will Not Go To Market Today
Anderson, Lena

Bunny Party
Anderson, Lena
  Bunny Story
Anderson, Lena
  Stina
Anderson, Lena
  Stina's Visit
Apple, Margot
  Blanket
Aragon, Jane Chelsea/Radzinski, Kandy
  Lullaby
Ardizzone, Edward
  Little Tim and the Brave Sea Captain
Ariane/Gusman, Annie
  Small Cloud
Arnold, Tedd
  No Jumping On The Bed
Arnosky, Jim
  Deer At The Brook
Arnosky, Jim
  Otters Under Water
Arnosky, Jim
  Raccoons and Ripe Corn
Arnosky, Jim
  Watching Foxes
Asch, Frank
  Moon Bear
Asch, Frank
  Mooncake
Auch, Mary Jane
  Peeping Beauty
Auch, Mary Jane
  The Easter Egg Farm
Aylesworth, Jim/Rand, Ted
  Country Crossing
Aylesworth, Jim/Gammell, Stephen
  Old Black Fly
Aylesworth, Jim/Frampton, David (woodcuts by)

My Son John
Baker, Alan
Two Tiny Mice
Baker, Keith
Hide And Snake
Baker, Leslie A.
The Third Story Cat
Bang, Molly
The Grey Lady and the Strawberry Snatcher
Bang, Molly
Yellow Ball
Barracca, Debra and Sal/Buehner, Mark
Maxi, The Hero
Barracca, Debra and Sal/Ayers, Alan
Maxi, The Star
Barracca, Debra and Sal/Buehner, Mark
The Adventures of Taxi Dog
Barton, Byron
Building A House
Baynton, Martin
Why Do You Love Me?
Bechtel, Beverly/Horvat, Laurel Moe
Lancelot The Ocelot
Bellamy, David/Dow, Jill
The Roadside
Bellamy, David/Dow, Jill
The Rock Pool
Bemelmans, Ludwig
Madeline
Berger, Barbara Helen
Grandfather Twilight
Berger, Barbara Helen
When The Sun Rose
Bester, Roger
Guess What?
Bilezikian, Gary
While I Slept
Blake, Quentin
Cockatoos
Bogaerts, Rascal and Gert
Socrates
Bonners, Susan

Just In Passing
Brandenberg, Franz/Aliki
Cock-A-Doodle-Doo
Brett, Jan
Annie and the Wild Animals
Brett, Jan
Christmas Trolls
Brett, Jan
Fritz and the Beautiful Horses
Brett, Jan
Goldilocks and the Three Bears
Brett, Jan
The First Dog
Brett, Jan
The Wild Christmas Reindeer
Brett, Jan
Trouble With Trolls
Briggs, Raymond
The Snowman
Brown, Marc
Arthur's Eyes
Brown, Marc
Arthur's Nose
Brown, Marc
Arthur's Tooth
Brown, Marc
D. W. Flips!
Brown, Marcia
Once A Mouse
Brown, Margaret Wise/Jeffers, Susan
Baby Animals
Brown, Margaret Wise/Bond, Felicia
Big Red Barn
Brown, Ruth
The Big Sneeze
Brown, Ruth
A Dark, Dark Tale
Brown, Ruth
I Don't Like It!
Brown, Ruth
Ladybug, Ladybug
Buckley, Richard/Carle, Eric
The Foolish Tortoise
Bucknall, Caroline

One Bear All Alone
Bulla, Clyde Robert/Ichikawa, Satomi
Keep Running, Allen!
Bunting, Eve/Brett, Jan
The Mother's Day Mice
Bunting, Eve/Meddaugh, Susan
No Nap
Burningham, John
Aldo
Burningham, John
Mr. Gumpy's Motor Car
Burningham, John
Mr. Gumpy's Outing
Burningham, John
Seasons
Burton, Virginia Lee
Katie and the Big Snow
Burton, Virginia Lee
The Little House
Burton, Virginia Lee
Mike Mulligan and His Steam Shovel
Bush, John/Geraghty, Paul
The Cross-With-Us Rhinoceros
Bush, John and Paul, Korky
The Fish Who Could Wish
Butler, Dorothy/Fuller, Elizabeth
My Brown Bear Barney
Butterworth, Nick
One Snowy Night
Butterworth, Nick & Inkpen, Mick
The Nativity Play
Cannon, Janell
Stellaluna
Carle, Eric
Do You Want To Be My Friend?
Carle, Eric
Have You Seen My Cat?
Carle, Eric
A House For Hermit Crab
Carle, Eric
Papa, Please Get The Moon For Me
Carle, Eric

Rooster's Off To See The World
Carle, Eric
The Secret Birthday Message
Carle, Eric
The Tiny Seed
Carle, Eric
The Very Busy Spider
Carle, Eric
The Very Hungry Caterpillar
Carle, Eric
The Very Quiet Cricket
Carlson, Nancy
Poor Carl
Carlstrom, Nancy White/Degen, Bruce
Better Not Get Wet, Jesse Bear
Carlstrom, Nancy White/Desimini, Lisa
Fish And Flamingo
Carlstrom, Nancy White/Kuroi, Ken
Swim The Silver Sea, Joshie Otter
Carlstrom, Nancy White/Nolan, Dennis
No Nap For Benjamin Badger
Carlstrom, Nancy White/Sorensen, Henri
What Does The Rain Play?
Catley, Alison
Jack's Basket
Cauley, Lorinda Bryan
The Pancake Boy
Cauley, Lorinda Bryan
The Town Mouse and the Country Mouse
Cazet, Denys
Christmas Moon
Cazet, Denys
Great Uncle Felix
Cazet, Denys
Mother Night
Chenery, Janet/Simont, Marc
Wolfie
Cherry, Lynne
Archie Follow Me
Chorao, Kay
Lemon Moon

Clements, Andrew/Yoshi
Big Al
Coats, Laura Jane
The Oak Tree
Coffelt, Nancy
Good Night, Sigmund
Cohen, Miriam/Hoban, Lillian
No Good In Art
Collington, Peter
The Angel and the Soldier Boy
Collington, Peter
Little Pickle
Collington, Peter
On Christmas Eve
Conover, Chris
Mother Goose and the Sly Fox
Conrad, Pam/Egielski, Richard
The Tub Grandfather
Conrad, Pam/Egielski, Richard
The Tub People
Cooney, Barbara
Miss Rumphius
Cooney, Nancy Evans/Hafner, Marylin
Chatterbox Jamie
Cooney, Nancy Evans/Mathis, Melissa Bay
The Umbrella Day
Crews, Donald
Ten Black Dots
Curtis, Gavin
Grandma's Baseball
Dale, Penny
Wake Up, Mr. B.!
Daly, Niki
Not So Fast Songololo
Day, Alexandra
Carl's Christmas
Day, Alexandra
Good Dog, Carl
Day, Alexandra
River Parade
Day, Betsy
Stefan And Olga
Demi
Demi's Opposites

Demi
Where Is It? A Hide-And-Seek Puzzle Book
dePaola, Tomie
Merry Christmas, Strega Nona
dePaola, Tomie
Nana Upstairs and Nana Downstairs
dePaola, Tomie
Pancakes For Breakfast
dePaola, Tomie
Now One Foot, Now The Other
dePaola, Tomie
Tom
dePaola, Tomie
Tomie dePaola's Favorite Nursery Tales
Dillon, Barbara/Conover, Chris
The Beast in the Bed
Dodd, Lynley
Slinky Malinki
Doherty, Berlie/O'Brien, Teresa
Paddiwak And Cozy
Donaldson, Julia/Scheffler, Axel
A Squash And A Sneeze
Downing, Julie
White Snow, Blue Feather
Dr. Seuss
500 Hats Of Bartholomew Cubbins
Dr. Seuss
Horton Hatches The Egg
Dr. Seuss
Horton Hears A Who!
Dragonwagon, Crescent/Pinkney, Jerry
Half A Moon and One Whole Star
Dunbar, Joyce/Majewska, Maria
Ten Little Mice
Ehlert, Lois
Eating the Alphabet - Fruits & Vegetables from A to Z
Ehlert, Lois
Feathers for Lunch
Ehlert, Lois

Fish Eyes - A Book You Can Count On
Ehlert, Lois
Nuts To You!
Finzel, Julia
Large As Life
Fleming, Denise
In The Small, Small Pond
Ernst, Lisa Campbell
Up To Ten and Down Again
Florian, Douglas
Nature Walk
Fox, Mem/Lofts, Pamela
Koala Lou
Frost, Robert/Jeffers, Susan
Stopping By Woods On A Snowy Evening
Fujikawa, Gyo
Can You Count?
Fujikawa, Gyo
A Child's Book Of Poems
Fyleman, Rose/Henterly, Jamichael
A Fairy Went A-Marketing
Gackenbach, Dick
Mighty Tree
Gackenbach, Dick
What's Claude Doing?
Galbraith, Kathryn O./Cooper, Floyd
Laura Charlotte
Gammell, Stephen
Once Upon MacDonald's Farm
Gantschev, Ivan
Otto the Bear
Garrison, Christian/Goode, Diane
The Dream Eater
Gauch, Patricia Lee/Ichikawa, Satomi
Dance, Tanya
Gay, Michel
Little Auto
Gay, Michel
Little Helicopter
Gay, Michel
Little Show
George, Lindsay Barrett
William and Boomer

George, William T./George, Lindsay Barrett
Box Turtle at Long Pond
Geraghty, Paul
Look Out, Patrick!
Gibbons, Gail
Clocks and How They Go
Gibbons, Gail
Fire! Fire!
Gibbons, Gail
From Seed to Plant
Gibbons, Gail
Locks and Keys
Gibbons, Gail
Sun Up, Sun Down
Giganti, Paul Jr./Crews, Donald
How Many Snails? A Counting Book
Gill, Madelaine
The Spring Hat
Goodman, Joan Elizabeth
Good Night, Pippin
Gould, Deborah/Harness, Cheryl
Aaron's Shirt
Graham, Bob
Grandad's Magic
Graham, Thomas
Mr. Bear's Chair
Gramatky, Hardie
Little Toot
Grifalconi, Ann
Darkness and the Butterfly
Griffit, Helen V./Tafuri, Nancy
Nata
Grimm Brothers/Watts, Bernadette
The Elves and the Shoemaker
Grindley, Sally/Dodds, Siobhan
Wake Up, Dad
Grossman, Virginia
Ten Little Rabbits
Guarino, Deborah/Kellogg, Steven
Is Your Mama A Llama
Guthrie, Donna/Hockerman, Dennis
A Rose for Abby
Haas, Irene

The Maggie B.
Hague, Kathleen/Hague, Michael
Numbears
Hague, Kathleen/Hague, Michael
Out Of The Nursery, Into The Night
Hartman, Gail/Stevenson, Harvey
As The Crow Flies
Hayes, Sarah/Ormerod, Jan
Eat Up, Gemma
Hayes, Sarah/Ormerod, Jan
Happy Christmas, Gemma
Heiligman, Deborah/Sweet, Melissa
Into The Night
Heine, Helme
Friends
Heine, Helme
The Marvelous Journey Through the Night
Heine, Helme
The Most Wonderful Egg In The World
Henkes, Kevin
All Alone
Henkes, Kevin
Bailey Goes Camping
Henkes, Kevin
Jessica
Hennessy, B. G./Carnabuci, Anthony
Sleep Tight
Hersom, Donald and Kathleen/Stock, Catherine
The Copycat
Hines, Anna Grossnickle
I'll Tell You What They Say
Hines, Anna Grossnickle
It's Just Me
Hines, Anna Grossnickle
Maybe A Band-Aid Will Help
Hirschi, Ron/Bash, Barbara
Forest
Hirschi, Ron/Bash, Barbara
Ocean
Hoban, Tana
Exactly the Opposite
Hoban, Tana
Of Color and Things
Hoban, Tana
Shadows and Reflections
Hoberman, Mary Ann/Fraser, Betty
A House Is A House For Me
Hoguet, Susan Ramsay
I Unpacked My Grandmother's Trunk
Hoopes, Lyn Littlefield/Watts, Trish Parcell
Half A Button
Howe, James/Young, Ed
I Wish I Were A Butterfly
Hudson, Cheryl Willis & Ford, Bernette G./Ford, George
Bright Eyes, Brown Skin
Hughes, Shirley
Alfie Gets In First
Hughes, Shirley
Alfie Gives A Hand
Hughes, Shirley
Alfie's Feet
Hughes, Shirley
Angel Mae
Hughes, Shirley
The Big Alfie and Annie Rose Storybook
Hughes, Shirley
The Big Alfie Out Of Doors Book
Hughes, Shirley
Dogger
Hughes, Shirley
An Evening At Alfie's
Hughes, Shirley
George the Babysitter
Hughes, Shirley
Good-Night, Owl!
Hutchins, Pat
The Surprise Party
Hutchins, Pat
Tidy Titch
Hutchins, Pat
What Game Shall We Play

Hutchins, Pat
Where's the Baby
Hutton, Warwick
Moses In The Bulrushes
Inkpen, Mick
If I Had A Sheep
Inkpen, Mick
Kipper
Inkpen, Mick
The Blue Balloon
Isadora, Rachel
Max
Iwamura, Kazuo
The Fourteen Forest Mice And The Harvest Moon Watch
Iwamura, Kazuo
Winter Sledding Day
Jeffers, Susan
All The Pretty Horses
Jeffers, Susan
Silent Night
Jensen, Helen Zane
When Panda Came To Our House
Johnson, Angela/Soman, David
Tell Me A Story, Mama
Johnson, Tony/dePaola, Tomie
The Quilt Story
Johnston, Tony/Hoban, Lillian
Little Bear Sleeping
Jonas, Ann
Reflections
Jonas, Ann
Round Trip
Jonas, Ann
The Trek
Jonas, Ann
Where Can It Be?
Jones, Carol (illustrated by)
This Old Man
Joyce, William
George Shrinks
Kantrowitz, Mildred/Parker, Nancy Winslow
Willy Bear

Karlin, Bernie and Mati/Karlin, Bernie
Night Ride
Keats, Ezra Jack
Peter's Chair
Keats, Ezra Jack
Regards To The Man In The Moon
Keats, Ezra Jack
Whistle For Willie
Keller, Holly
Geraldine's Blanket
Kellogg, Steven
Can I Keep Him?
Kellogg, Steven
The Mystery of the Missing Red Mitten
Kerr, Judith
Mog and Bunny
Killion, Bette/Falk, Barbara Bustetter
The Same Wind
King, Deborah
Cloudy
Kitameira, Satoshi
When Sheep Cannot Sleep - The Counting Book
Kitchen, Bert
Animal Numbers
Korschunow, Irina/Michl, Reinhard
The Foundling Fox
Krahn, Fernando
The Biggest Christmas Tree On Earth
Krahn, Fernando
The Self-Made Snowman
Kraus, Robert/Aruego, Jose and Dewey, Ariane
Where Are You Going Little Mouse?
Kraus, Robert/Aruego, Jose
Whose Mouse Are You?
Lakin, Patricia/Brewster, Patience
Don't Touch My Room
Leaf, Munro/Lawson, Robert
The Story of Ferdinand
Leedy, Loreen

A Number of Dragons
Lester, Alison
Clive Eats Alligators
Lester, Helen/Munsinger, Lynn
Me First
Lewis, Rob
Tidy Up, Trevor
Lewison, Wendy Cheyette/Wijngaard, Juan
Going To Sleep On The Farm
Lindbergh, Reeve/Kellogg, Steven
The Day the Goose Got Loose
Lindbergh, Reeve/Jeffers, Susan
The Midnight Farm
Lionni, Leo
A Color Of His Own
Lionni, Leo
It's Mine!
Lionni, Leo
Swimmy
Lobel, Anita
Sven's Bridge
Lobel, Arnold/Lobel, Anita
The Rose In My Garden
London, Jonathan/Rand, Ted
The Owl Who Became The Moon
Lottridge, Celia Barker/Wallace, Ian
The Name of the Tree
Lucas, Barbara/Ormai, Stella
Sleeping Over
Ludwig, Warren
Good Morning, Granny Rose
MacCarthy, Patricia
Animals Galore!
MacDonald, Amy/Fox-Davies, Sarah
Little Beaver and The Echo
McDonald, Megan/Schindler, S. D.
Whoo-oo Is It?
MacDonald, Suse
Alphabatics
Maddern, Eric/Kennaway, Adrienne
Curious Clownfish
Maestro, Betsy and Giulio
Delivery Van

Mahy, Margaret/MacCarthy, Patricia
17 Kings And 42 Elephants
Manushkin, Fran/DeGroat, Diane
Little Rabbit's Baby Brother
Marion, Jeff Daniel/Bowman, Leslie
Hello Crow
Maris, Ron
Bernard's Boring Day
Marshall, James
Hansel and Gretel
Martin, Bill Jr. and Archambault, John/Ehlert, Lois
Chicka Chicka Boom Boom
Martin, Jerome
Carrot/Parrot
Martin, Jerome
Mitten/Kitten
Mason, Ann Maree/Wilcox, Cathy
The Weird Things In Nanna's House
Mayer, Mercer
A Boy, A Dog and A Frog
Mayer, Mercer
Frog Goes To Dinner
Mayer, Mercer
Frog On His Own
Mayer, Mercer
Frog, Where Are You?
Mayer, Mercer
Hiccup
Mayer, Mercer
Just For You
Mayer, Mercer
Just Go To Bed
Mayer, Mercer
Terrible Troll
Mayer, Mercer
There's A Nightmare In My Closet
Mayer, Mercer
There's An Alligator Under My Bed
Mayer, Mercer and Marianna
A Boy, A Dog, A Frog and A Friend

McCloskey, Robert
One Morning In Maine
McDonald, Megan/Schindler, S. D.
Is This A House for Hermit Crab?
McLeod, Emilie Warren/McPhail, David
The Bear's Bicycle
McNulty, Faith/Marstall, Bob
The Lady and the Spider
McPhail, David
Adam's Smile
McPhail, David
The Bear's Toothache
McPhail, David
The Dream Child
McPhail, David
Emma's Pet
McPhail, David
First Flight
McPhail, David
Fix-It
McPhail, David
Great Cat
McPhail, David
The Party
McPhail, David
Something Special
Merriam, Eve/de Groat, Diane
Where Is Everybody?
Merriam, Eve/Karlin, Bernie
12 Ways To Get To 11
Mezek, Karen
Christmas At Rumpole Mansion
Miles, Sally/Cain, Errol Le
Alfi And The Dark
Morel, Eve/Fujikawa, Gyo
Fairy Tales and Fables
Morozumi, Atsuko
One Gorilla
Morris, Neil/Stevenson, Peter
Rummage Sale A Fun Book Of Shapes And Colors
Muller, Gerda

The Garden In The City
Novak, Matt
Rolling
Ochs, Carol Partridge/Redenbaugh, Vicki Jo
When I'm Alone
Oppenheim, Joanne/Litzinger, Rosanne
The Story Book Prince
Ormerod, Jan
Moonlight
Ormerod, Jan
Rhymes Around The Day
Ormerod, Jan
The Story Of Chicken Licken
Ormerod, Jan
When We Went To The Zoo
Ormerod, Jan
Young Joe
Ormondroyd, Edward/Larrecq, John M.
Theodore
Oxenbury, Helen
First Day Of School
Oxenbury, Helen
When I'm Sleepy
Pederson, Judy
The Tiny Patient
Peet, Bill
The Whingdingdilly
Pelham, David
A Is For Animals - An Animal ABC
Pike, Norman/De Witt, Robin and Patricia
The Peach Tree
Pilcher, Steve
Elfabit
Polacco, Patricia
Thunder Cake
Potter, Beatrix
The Tale Of Peter Rabbit
Prater, John
The Gift
Pringle, Laurence/Morrill, Leslie Holt
Jesse Builds A Road
Provensen, Alice and Martin

Our Animals At Maple Hill Farm
Paxton, Tom/Ingraham, Erick
The Animals Lullaby
Pfister, Marcus/James, J. Alison
(translated by)
The Rainbow Fish
Polacco, Patricia
The Bee Tree
Price, Moe/Morozumi, Atsuko
The Reindeer Christmas
Provensen, Alice & Martin
The Year At Maple Hill Farm
Pryor, Bonnie/de Groat, Diane
Amanda and April
Pryor, Bonnie/Graham, Mark
Greenbrook Farm
Raschka,Chris
Yo! Yes?
Ray, Deborah Kogan
Stargazing Sky
Rayner, Mary
Garth Pig Steals The Show
Rayner, Mary
The Rain Cloud
Reiser, Lynne
Tomorrow On Rocky Pond
Remkiewicz, Frank
The Last Time I Saw Harris
Riddell, Chris
The Trouble With Elephants
Robins, Joan/Hafner, Marylin
My Brother, Will
Roe, Eileen/Cogancherry, Helen
All I Am
Roffey, Maureen
I Spy On Vacation
Root, Phyllis/Sandford, John
The Old Red Rocking Chair
Rotner, Shelley and Kreisler, Ken/
Rotner, Shelley
Ocean Day
Rounds, Glen
Cowboys
Russo, Marisabina

The Line Up Book
Ryder, Joanne/Bolognese, Don
Fireflies
Ryder, Joanne/Bonforte, Lisa
Animals In The Wood
Ryder, Joanne/Cherry, Lynn
Chipmunk Song
Ryder, Joanne/Cherry, Lynne
The Snail's Spell
Ryder, Joanne/Owens, Gail
Fog In The Meadow
Ryder, Joanne/Cherry, Lynne
The Snail's Spell
Ryder, Joanne/Harness, Cheryl
Under the Moon
Ryder, Joanne/Nolan, Dennis
Under Your Feet
Ryder, Joanne/Cherry, Lynne
Where Butterflies Grow
Scamell, Ragnhild/Hobson, Sally
Three Bags Full
Scheffler, Ursel/Wensell, Ulises
A Walk In The Rain
Schermbrucker, Reviva/Daly, Niki
Charlie's House
Schories, Pat
Mouse Around
Schubert, Dieter
Where's My Monkey
Scott, Ann Herbet/Coalson, Glo
On Mother's Lap
Sendak, Maurice
Where The Wild Things Are
Serfozo, Mary/Narahashi, Keiko
Rain Talk
Siberell, Anne
Whale In The Sky
Siebert, Diane/Wimmer, Mike
Train Song
Sis, Peter
Beach Ball
Sis, Peter
Going Up! - A Color Counting Book
Sis, Peter

Komodo!
Skorpen, Liesel M./Sandin, Joan
Michael
Smee, Nicola
The Tusk Fairy
Snyder, Dianne/Say, Allen
The Boy Of The Three Year Nap
Spier, Peter
Noah's Ark
Spier, Peter
Peter Spier's Rain
Stanley, Diane
Fiddle-I-Fee
Steptoe, John
The Story of Jumping Mouse
Stepto, Michele/Himmelman, John
Snuggle Piggy And The Magic Blanket
Stevens, Janet
Goldilocks and the Three Bears
Stevens, Janet
The Three Billy Goats Gruff
Stevenson, James
Grandpa's Too-Good Garden
Stevenson, James
No Friends
Stevenson, James
We Can't Sleep
Stevenson, James
Will You Please Feed Our Cat?
Stevenson, Robert Louis/Wolff, Ashley
Block City
Stock, Catherine
Sophie's Bucket
Stock, Catherine
Secret Valentine
Stock, Catherine
Sophie's Knapsack
Szekeres, Cyndy (illustrated by) Lanes, Selma G. (selected and adapted by)
Cyndy Szekeres' Book Of Nursery Tales
Tafuri, Nancy

Do Not Disturb
Tafuri, Nancy
Junglewalk
Tafuri, Nancy
Who's Counting?
Taylor, Kim and Burton, Jane (photographed by)
Frog
Tejima, Keisaburo
The Bears' Autumn
Tejima, Keisaburo
Fox's Dream
Tejima, Keisaburo
Owl Lake
Tejima, Keisaburo
Swan Sky
Tejima, Keisaburo
Woodpecker Forest
Thayer, Jane/McCue, Lisa
The Popcorn Dragon
Thornhill, Jan
The Wildlife 1.2.3 A Nature Counting Book
Titherington, Jeanne
A Place For Ben
Titherington, Jeanne
Where Are You Going, Emma?
Tobias, Tobi/Swafford, Jeanette
The Dawdlewalk
Tompert, Ann/Mursinger, Lynn
Just A Little Bit
Tresselt, Alvin/Ewing, Carolyn
Wake Up Farm!
Tresselt, Alvin/Ewing, Carolyn
Wake Up, City!
Tresselt, Alvin/Yaroslava
The Mitten
Tryon, Leslie
Albert's Alphabet
Turkle, Brinton
Deep In The Forest
Valiska, Gregory/Munsinger, Lynn
Babysitting For Benjamin
Van Der Beek, Deborah
Superbabe

Van Laan, Nancy/Booth, George
Possum Come A-Knockin'
Van Lann, Nancy/Meade, Holly
This Is The Hat
verDorn, Bethea/Graham, Thomas
Day Breaks
Viorst, Judith/Chorao, Kay
The Good-bye Book
Waber, Bernard
The House On East 88th Street
Waddell, Martin/Mansell, Dom
My Great Grandpa
Waddell, Martin/Firth, Barbara
The Park In the Dark
Wagner, Jenny
Aranea, A Story About A Spider
Wahl, Jan/Joyce, William
Humphrey's Bear
Wallace, Barbara Brooks/Sandford, John
Argyle
Walsh, Ellen Stoll
Mouse Paint
Watt, Barrie (photographed by)
Duck
Weir, Alison
Peter, Good Night
Weisner, David
Free Fall
Weiss, Nicki
An Egg Is An Egg
Weiss, Nicki
Barney Is Big
Weiss, Nicki
Waiting
Weiss, Nicki
Where Does the Brown Bear Go?
Wellington, Monica
Seasons Of Swans
Wells, Rosemary
A Lion For Lewis
Wells, Rosemary
First Tomato - A Voyage To The Bunny Planet
Wells, Rosemary
Hazel's Amazing Mother
Wells, Rosemary
Max's Chocolate Chicken
Wells, Rosemary
Moss Pillows - A Voyage To The Bunny Planet
Wells, Rosemary
Shy Charles
Wells, Rosemary
The Island Light - A Voyage To The Bunny Planet
Wells, Rosemary
Timothy Goes To School
Whatley, Bruce
Looking For Crabs
Wildsmith, Brian
Brian Wildsmith's 1, 2, 3's
Wildsmith, Brian
Brian Wildsmith's ABC
Wildsmith, Brian
Brian Wildsmith's Fishes
Wildsmith, Brian
Goat's Trail
Wilhelm, Hans
Tyronne The Horrible
Williams, Vera B.
Cherries and Cherry Pits
Winter, Paula
Sir Andrew
Winthrop, Elizabeth/Brewster, Patience
Bear and Mrs. Duck
Wolff, Ashley
A Year of Birds
Wood, Audrey/Wood, Don
King Bidgood's In The Bathtub
Wood, Audrey/Wood, Don
The Napping House
Yabuuchi, Masayuki
Animals Sleeping
Yabuuchi, Masayuki
Whose Baby?
Yabuuchi, Masayuki

School-Age

School-Age

OBSERVING THE SCHOOL-AGE CHILD

A new era dawns when children enter school. They now begin the years of formal education and their reaction to it and success with it in the early years often sets the pace for the next 12 or more years. The most outstanding academic achievements in their early school years will be learning to read, write and understand number concepts. If they feel confident and successful in these areas, they are more likely to have a positive attitude about school than if they are frustrated or see themselves as "not as smart" as the rest of the children in the class.

Each child is unique with his or her interests, likes and dislikes becoming more varied and diverse each year. School children can at one moment be pictures of self-confidence and security and the next moment be shedding tears because they don't understand something. They long to be part of the group — to belong. They treasure a few close friends though these may change from day to day. The social aspect of their lives grows in importance as they get older.

WHAT PARENTS CAN DO

Parents of kindergartners and first-graders have an important job as their children begin the work of learning to read. Traditionally, reading readiness skills such as letter sounds and left-to-right visual patterns were taught in kindergarten and actual reading began in first grade, but some schools today are teaching reading as early as kindergarten. Whenever it begins, the parent's job is not to teach "how" to read (knowing letter sounds is helpful if your child asks) but instead to provide the practice time, to motivate, to keep the love of books alive by continuing daily read-aloud time, and to have lots of conversations.

Because reading skills improve by practicing those skills, set aside time each day to listen to your child read. Even when children are already reading when they enter school, it still takes work and time to progress to a higher level. Children as well as parents are sometimes surprised at how long it takes to become a truly proficient reader and they can become discouraged. Keep in mind that the teaching of reading continues all through elementary school and true absorption, being totally lost to the world while curled up with a book, usually doesn't occur until well into 3rd or 4th grade. A warm, accepting atmosphere, encouraging words, and honest praise for each accomplishment as well as non-stressful but routine practice time will help immeasurably to build skills as well as confidence.

In second grade, children refine their reading skills. Fluency, the skill of reading smoothly and with expression, usually develops sometime between the end of first grade and the end of second. When a child becomes fluent, his primary task shifts from working on decoding the words to finding meaning in the words and story. Talking with your child about the story builds these comprehension skills. Talk about what you read aloud and what your child reads. Use science or social studies books or choose interesting newspaper articles to read aloud (not too frightening or adult). Early school-age children are fascinated with what goes on in the world and, with encouragement, will form their own opinions.

Beware, though, children are quick to recognize and many will "tune out" questions that are too close to test-type (questions with one right answer). For example:

How did Tom get out of white-washing the fence?
Who were Charlotte's barnyard friends?
Why was Black Beauty's first owner forced to sell him?

It's clear here that there is one right answer and, once it is answered, there's not much more to be said. Compare with:

I can't decide if Tom was more lazy or more clever. What do you think?

Can we think of other ways Charlotte and the rest of the animals could have saved Wilbur?
Do you think Ginger was a good friend to Black Beauty?

The answers to these questions can be varied and, if the topics are interesting to everyone involved, can lead to some interesting discussions. The more your questions or comments reflect things you yourself truly wonder about, the less contrived your conversations will sound and the more likely you'll start your child thinking and talking. As always, don't pressure or force answers. If your youngster feels he's not measuring up or the situation is stressful, it will do far more harm than good.

THE SCHOOL-AGE CHILD AND BOOKS

Children in kindergarten and first grade make up an enjoyable age-group to read to. They enjoy a wide variety of books and they are enthusiastic listeners. They still love picture books and will enjoy many titles from their preschool years because now they bring more advanced understanding to the experience. They can catch subtle meanings or humor they missed when they were younger. They are ready for a great many additional picture books with more involved character development and vocabulary as well as chapter books such as *Socks* and *Ramona the Pest* by Beverly Cleary or *The Stories Julian Tells* by Ann Cameron.

Second and third graders are in a stage of weaning from picture books to chapter books. Picture books, of course, will continue to hold much appeal for children for a number of years (after all we as adults are often surprised at how much we enjoy them).

Children in the third grade become increasingly confident and independent in their reading, and by the fourth grade most can read with ease many books which hold high interest for them. For many children, the fourth grade is a turning point. Some move on to become absorbed readers, while others lose interest in reading. Too often other interests such as television viewing, extracurricular activities and social interests take precedence and children can pass through this age without acquiring a true love for reading.

Parents can help the child maintain a balance among a variety of activities and experiences and need to be alert for signs that the child's interest in books is waning. When they see children slipping away from books, extra effort may be needed to find appealing books, to take excursions to spark new interests or renew old ones, or to call upon their creativity to draw the children back into reading.

TIPS FOR PARENTS OF SCHOOL-AGE CHILDREN

1. Have your child's eyes checked not only for acuity but also for tracking and focusing. These tests are often not routinely done, but many difficulties experienced by beginning readers can be traced to problems in tracking and focusing.
2. Read aloud books with vocabulary rich in description and imagery.
3. When the beginning reader selects a book to read aloud, it sometimes helps if you read it aloud to him first.
4. Try alternating reading — you read a page and your child reads a page.
5. Try reading aloud in unison.
6. There may be times when your child resists reading. One mother offered a ticket for every book completed. The tickets were accumulated and then traded for purchasing a book. (You'll have ideas even better than this. Try them!)
7. School-age children may have favorite authors and illustrators. Check out other books by these authors and artists.
8. Continue to read aloud even when the child is reading. Listening vocabulary is three to four years ahead of speaking and reading vocabulary.

Grades 1 & 2 Booklist

Aardema, Verna/Dillon, Leo and Diane
Who's In Rabbit's House?
Aardema, Verna/Dillon, Leo and Diane
Why Mosquitoes Buzz in People's Ears
Abercrombie, Barbara/Graham, Mark
Charlie Anderson
Ackerman, Karen/Weinhaus, Karen Ann
Flannery Row
Ackerman, Karen/Gammell, Stephen
Song and Dance Man
Ahlberg, Janet and Allan
The Jolly Postman
Alderson, Sue Ann/Blades, Ann
Ida and the Wool Smugglers
Alexander, Lloyd/Keats, Ezra Jack
The King's Fountain
Alexander, Sue/Christelow, Eileen
Dear Phoebe
Aliki
The Two Of Them
Allard, Harry/Marshall, James
Miss Nelson Is Back
Allard, Harry/Marshall, James
Miss Nelson Is Missing
Allen, Jeffrey/Marshall, James
Nosey Mrs. Rat
Allen, Judy/Humphries, Tudor
Tiger

Andersen, Hans Christian/Vaes, Alain
The Steadfast Tin Soldier
Andrews, Jan/Wallace, Ian
Very Last First Time
Anno, Mitsumasa
Anno's Alphabet
Anno, Mitsumasa
Anno's Counting Book
Anno, Mitsumasa
Anno's Journey
Arnosky, Jim
I Was Born In A Tree And Raised By Bees
Aruego, Jose & Dewey, Ariane
We Hide, You Seek
Asch, Frank/Vagin, Vladimir
Here Comes the Cat!
Aylesworth, Jim/Goffe, Toni
Mother Halverson's New Cat
Baker, Jeannie
Grandfather
Baker, Jeannie
Home In The Sky
Baker, Keith
The Magic Fan
Baker, Keith
Who is the Beast?
Balian, Lorna
The Aminal
Barker, Marjorie/Yoshi
Magical Hands
Barnhart, Peter/Adams, Adrienne
The Wounded Duck
Barrett, Judi/Barrett, Ron
Animals Should Definitely Not Wear Clothes
Barrett, Judi/Barrett, Ron
Cloudy With A Chance Of Meatballs
Barrett, Judi
A Snake Is Totally Tail
Bartone, Elisa/Lewin, Ted
Peppe The Lamplighter

Bauer, Caroline Feller/Paterson, Diane
Too Many Books
Bedard, Michael/Cooney, Barbara
Emily
Bemelmans, Ludwig
Madeline
Berenzy, Alix
A Frog Prince
Blos, Joan W./Gammell, Stephen
Old Henry
Bolliger, Max/O'Brist, Jurg
The Lonely Prince
Bond, Felicia
Poinsettia And Her Family
Borton, Lady/Ray, Deborah Kogan
Fat Chance
Bourke, Linda
Eye Spy - A Mysterious Alphabet
Bozylinsky, Hannah Heritage
Lala Salama An African Lullaby
Brett, Jan
Beauty and the Beast
Brett, Jan
Berlioz
Brett, Jan
The Twelve Days of Christmas
Brown, Marc
Arthur Babysits
Brown, Craig
The Patchwork Farmer
Brown, Marc
The True Francine
Brown, Ruth
If at First You Do Not See
Bulla, Clyde Robert/Charlot, Jean
The Poppy Seeds
Bulla, Clyde/Hyman, Trina
The Moon Singer
Bunting, Eve/Peck, Beth
How Many Days to America?
Bunting, Eve/Rand, Ted
Night Tree
Bunting, Eve/Himler, Ronald

Someday A Tree
Bunting, Eve/Peck, Beth
The Day Before Christmas
Bunting, Eve/Carrick, Donald
The Wednesday Surprise
Burningham, John
Come Away From The Water, Shirley
Burningham, John
John Patrick Norman McHennessy - The Boy Who Was Always Late
Burningham, John
Where's Julius
Burningham, John
Would You Rather
Butterworth, Nick and Inkpen, Mick
The School Trip
Byars, Betsy/McCully, Emily A.
Go And Hush The Baby
Cameron, Ann/Strugnell, Ann
Julian, Dream Doctor
Cameron, Ann/Allison, Diane
Julian, Secret Agent
Cameron, Ann/Leder, Dora
Julian's Glorious Summer
Cameron, Ann/Strugnell, Ann
More Stories Julian Tells
Cameron, Ann
The Most Beautiful Place in the World
Cameron, Ann/Strugnell, Ann
The Stories Julian Tells
Carlson, Nancy
Take Time To Relax
Carlstrom, Nancy
Arnie and the New Kid
Carlstrom, Nancy White/Molk, Láurel
Grandpappy
Carrick, Carol/Carrick, Donald
Patrick's Dinosaurs
Carrick, Carol/Carrick, Donald
Stay Away From Simon
Carrick, Carol/Carrick, Donald
What Happened To Patrick's

Dinosaurs
Carson, Jo/Downing, Julie
Pulling My Leg
Caseley, Judith
When Grandpa Came to Stay
Castle, Caroline/Weavers, Peter
The Hare and the Tortoise
Caudill, Rebecca/Ness, Evaline
A Pocketful of Cricket
Cauley, Lorinda Bryan
The Cock, The Mouse And The Little Red Hen
Cazet, Denys
A Fish in His Pocket
Cazzola, Gus/Morgan, Pierr
The Bells Of Santa Lucia
Chambless, Jane
Tucker and the Bear
Chapman, Carol/Kellogg, Steven
Barney Bipple's Magic Dandelions
Cheh, John/Nally, Sharon McGinley
My Grandmother's Journey
Cherry, Lynne
The Great Kapok Tree
Chetwin, Grace/Small, David
Box and Cox
Chorao, Kay
Cathedral Mouse
Chorao, Kay
Molly's Lies
Cleary, Beverly/Darling, Louis
Beezus and Ramona
Cleary, Beverly/Darling, Louis
Ellen Tebbits
Cleary, Beverly/Darling, Louis
Henry and Beezus
Cleary, Beverly/Darling, Louis
Henry and Ribsy
Cleary, Beverly/Darling, Louis
Henry Huggins
Cleary, Beverly/Darling, Louis
The Mouse and the Motorcycle
Cleary, Beverly/Zelinsky, Paul O.
Ralph S. Mouse

Cleary, Beverly/Darling, Louis
Runaway Ralph
Cleary, Beverly/Darwin, Beatrice
Socks
Clifton, Lucille/Grifalconi, Ann
Everett Anderson's Goodbye
Climo, Shirley/Heller, Ruth
The Korean Cinderella
Cohen, Barbara/Cuffari, Richard
Thank You, Jackie Robinson
Cohen, Miriam
No Good in Art
Cohen, Miriam/Hoban, Lillian
Will I Have A Friend?
Cole, Joanna/Duke, Kate
Don't Tell The Whole World!
Cook, Joel
The Rats' Daughter
Cooney, Barbara
Little Brother and Little Sister
Cowcher, Helen
Tigress
Cox, David
Bossyboots
Craft, Ruth/Haas, Irene
Carrie Hepple's Garden
Croll, Carolyn
The Little Snowgirl
Croll, Carolyn (adapted and illustrated)
The Three Brothers
Czernecki, Stefan and Rhodes, Timothy/Czernecki, Stefan
The Sleeping Bread
Daly, Niki
Papa Lucky's Shadow
Damrell, Liz/Marchesi, Stephen
With The Wind
de Hamel, Joan/Ross, Christine
Hemi's Pet
Demi
The Empty Pot
Denslow, Sharon/Carpenter, Nancy
At Taylor's Place
Denslow, Sharon Phillips/Kastner, Jill
Night Owls

dePaola, Tomie
Charlie Needs A Cloak
dePaola, Tomie
Jamie O'Rourke And The Big Potato
dePaola, Tomie
Jingle The Christmas Clown
dePaola, Tomie
Merry Christmas Strega Nona
dePaola, Tomie
Now One Foot, Now The Other
dePaola, Tomie
The Knight and the Dragon
Denslow, Sharon Phillips/Carpenter, Nancy
Bus Riders
Dickens, Charles/Mayer, Mercer
A Christmas Carol - Being a Ghost Story of Christmas
Doherty, Berlie/O'Brien, Teresa
Paddiwak and Cozy
Dragonwagon, Crescent/Pinkney, Jerry
Home Place
Dunbar, Fiona
You'll Never Guess!
Dunphy, Madeleine/Robinson, Alan James
Here Is The Arctic Winter
Dunrea, Olivier
Eppie M. Says . . .
Edwards, Michelle
Chicken Man
Egger, Bettina/Jucker, Sita
Marianne's Grandmother
Engel, Diana
Josephina Hates Her Name
Engel, Diana
Josephina the Great Collector
Ernst, Lisa Campbell
Nettie Parsons' Good-Luck Lamb
Ernst, Lisa Campbell
Sam Johnson and the Blue Ribbon Quilt
Ernst, Lisa Campbell

Squirrel Park
Ernst. Lisa Campbell
Zinnia And Dot
Esbensen, Barbara J./Davis, Helen K.
The Star Maiden
Fair, Sylvia
The Bedspread
Fisher, Leonard Everett
Sailboat Lost
Fleischman, Paul/Beddows, Eric
Shadow Play
Flournoy, Valerie/Pinkney, Jerry
The Patchwork Quilt
Forest, Heather (retold)/Gaber, Susan
The Woman Who Flummoxed the Fairies
Forrester, Victoria/Boulet, Susan Seddon
Poor Gabriella - A Christmas Story
Fox, Mem/Denton, Terry
Night Noises
Fox, Mem/Mullins, Patricia
Shoes From My Grandpa
Fox, Mem/Vivas,Julie
Wilfrid Gordan McDonald Partridge
Gackenbach, Dick
Beauty, Brave and Beautiful
Gammell, Stephen
Git Along, Old Scudder
Garrison, Christian/Goode, Diane
The Dream Eater
Gellman, Ellie/Friedman, Judith
Jeremy's Dreidel
Gerstein, Mordecai
The Seal Mother
Goble,Paul
Dream Wolf
Goble, Paul
Her Seven Brothers
Goble, Paul
Iktomi And The Boulder
Goffstein, M. B.
Our Snowman

Goldin, Barbara Diamon/Weihs, Erika
Cakes And Miracles
Goodall, John S.
Puss In Boots
Gray, Libba Moore/Rowland, Jada
Miss Tizzy
Greaves, Margaret/Gooding, Beverley
Once There Were No Pandas
Greenfield, Eloise/Byard, Carole
African Dream
Greenfield, Eloise/Cooper, Floyd
Grandpa's Face
Grifalconi, Ann
Osa's Pride
Grifalconi, Ann
The Village Of The Round And Square Houses
Griffith, Helen V./Smith, Jos. A.
"Mine Will," Said John
Grimm Brothers/Marks, Alan
The Fisherman and His Wife
Grimm Brothers, Randall, Jerrell/Zemach, Margot
The Fisherman and His Wife
Grimm Brothers/Ursell, Martin
The Golden Goose
Grimm Brothers/Jeffers, Susan
Hansel And Gretel
Grimm Brothers/Hague, Michael
Rapunzel
Grimm, Brothers/Cain, Errol Le
The Twelve Dancing Princesses
Harshman, Marc and Collins, Bonnie/Goffe, Toni
Rocks In My Pockets
Haseley, Dennis/Wiesner, David
Kite Flier
Havill, Juanita/O'Brien, Ann Sibley
Jamaica's Find
Heide, Florence Parry and Gilliland, Judith   Heide/Lewin, Ted
The Day of Ahmed's Secret
Heine, Helme
The Pearl
Henkes, Kevin

Chester's Way
Henkes, Kevin
Chrysanthemum
Henkes, Kevin
Grandpa & Bo
Henkes, Kevin
Sheila Rae, The Brave
Henkes, Kevin
A Weekend With Wendell
Hennessy, B. G./Pearson, Tracey Campbell
School Days
Herriot, James
Blossom Comes Home
Herriot, James
Bonny's Big Day
Herriot,James
Only One Woof
Herriot, James/Brown, Ruth
Oscar, Cat-About-Town
Herriot, James/Brown, Ruth
The Christmas Day Kitten
Hesse, Karen/Carpenter, Nancy
Lester's Dog
Hewett, Joan/Carrick, Donald
Rosalie
Heyward, Du Bose/Flack, Marjorie
The Country Bunny and the Little Gold Shoes
Hill, Elizabeth Starr/Speidel, Sandra
Evan's Corner
Hilton, Nette/Power, Margaret
The Long Red Scarf
Hiser, Berniece/Szilagyi, Mary
Charlie and His Wheat Straw Hat
Hoffman, Mary/Binch, Caroline
Amazing Grace
Holabird, Katharine/Craig, Helen
Angelina and Alice
Holabird, Katharine
Angelina and The Princess
Holabird, Katharine/Craig, Helen
Angelina's Christmas
Hopkinson, Deborah/Ransome,

The Rumor of Pavel and Paali
Knutson, Barbara
    How the Guinea Fowl Got Her Spots
Komaiko, Leah/Cornell, Laura
    Annie Bananie
Kovalski, Maryann
    Pizza For Breakfast
Krahn, Fernando
    April Fools
Kraus, Robert
    Leo The Late Bloomer
Kraus, Robert/Aruego, Jose and Dewey, Ariane
    Owliver
Krause, Ute
    Nora and the Great Bear
Kroll, Steven/Carrick, Donald
    Big Jeremy
LaRochelle, David/Skoro, Martin
    A Christmas Guest
Lenski, Lois
    Strawberry Girl
Lesser, Carolyn/Cauley, Lorinda Bryan
    The Goodnight Circle
Lewin, Ted
    Amazon Boy
Lewis, J. Patrick/Zimmer, Dirk
    The Moonbow Of Mr. B. Bones
Lindbergh, Reeve/Kellogg, Steven
    The Day The Goose Got Loose
Lindgren, Astrid/Wiberg, Harald
    The Tomten
Lindgren, Astrid/Wiberg, Harald
    The Tomten and the Fox
Lionni, Leo
    Frederick
Lobel, Arnold
    Ming Lo Moves The Mountain
Lobel, Arnold/Lobel, Anita
    How The Rooster Saved The Day
Lobel, Arnold/Lobel, Anita
    On Market Street
Lobel, Arnold/Lobel, Anita

The Rose In My Garden
London, Jonathan/Sauber, Robert
    Gray Fox
Longfellow, Henry Wadsworth/Jeffers, Susan
    Hiawatha
Luttrell, Ida/McDermott, Michael
    Three Good Blankets
Lyon, George Ella/Szilagyi, Mary
    Basket
Lyon, George Ella/Gammell, Stephen
    Come A Tide
Lyon, George Ella/Catalanotto, Peter
    Who Came Down That Road?
MacLachlan, Patricia/Pertzoff, Alexander
    Three Names
Mahy, Margaret/Tseng, Jean and Mousien
    The Seven Chinese Brothers
Mansell, Dom
    If Dinsosaurs Came To Town
Manson, Christopher
    Two Travelers
Marshall, Edward/Marshall, James
    Troll Country
Martin, Bill Jr. and Archambault, John/Rand, Ted
    Knots On A Counting Rope
Martin, Bill Jr. and Archambault, John/Rand, Ted
    Barn Dance!
Martin, Charles E.
    For Rent
Martin, Jacqueline Briggs/Gaber, Susan
    Good Times On Grandfather Mountain
Mayer, Mercer
    Liza Lou and the Yeller Belly Swamp
Marzollo, Jean/Wick, Walter (photographs)
    I Spy Christmas
McCully, Emily Arnold
    Mirette On The High Wire

McCully, Emily Arnold
New Baby
McCully, Emily Arnold
School
McCully, Emily Arnold
The Christmas Gift
McKissack, Patricia C./Isadora, Rachel
Flossie and the Fox
McKissack, Patricia/Cook, Scott
Nettie Jo's Friends
McKissack, Patricia/Pinkney, Jerry
Mirandy and Brother Wind
McDonald, Megan/Lewin, Ted
The Great Pumpkin Switch
McKissack, Patricia C./Schutzer, Dena
A Million Fish . . . More Or Less
McMillan, Bruce
Mouse Views: What The Class Pet Saw
Merriam, Eve/Graves, Linda
The Wise Woman And Her Secret
Merriam,Eve/Small, David
The Christmas Box
Mikolaycak, Charles
Babushka
Miller, Edna
Jumping Bean
Mitchell. Margaree King/Ransome, James
Uncle Jed's Barbershop
Moore, Elaine/Primavera, Elise
Grandma's House
Moore, Elaine/Primavera, Elise
Grandma's Promise
Morris, Winifred/Chen, Ju Hong
The Magic Leaf
Murphy, Shirley Rousseau/dePaola, Tomie
Tattie's River Journey
Newfield, Marcia/DaRif, Andrea
Where Did You Put Your Sleep?
Noble, Trinka Hakes

Apple Tree Christmas
Noble, Trinka Hakes/Kellogg, Steven
The Day Jimmy's Boa Ate The Wash
Nordqvist, Sven
Merry Christmas, Festus and Mercury
Nordqvist, Sven
Pancake Pie
Nordqvist, Sven
The Fox Hunt
Nordqvist, Sven
Wishing To Go Fishing
Nunes, Susan/Himler, Ronald
Coyote Dreams
Oakley, Graham
The Church Mice And The Ring
Okimoto, Jean Davies/Schneider, Howie
Blumpoe the Grumpoe Meets Arnold The Cat
Paraskevas, Betty/Paraskevas, Michael
The Strawberry Dog
Parish, Peggy/Siebel, Fritz
Amelia Bedelia
Parnall, Peter
Quiet
Passen, Lisa
Fat, Fat Rose Marie
Patrick, Denise Lewis/Ransome, James
Red Dancing Shoes
Paxton, Tom/Kellogg, Steven
Engelbert the Elephant
Peet, Bill
Cock-A-Doodle Dudley
Peet, Bill
Pamela Camel
Peet, Bill
Zella, Zack and Zodiac
Perrault, Charles/Marcellino, Fred
Puss In Boots
Pike, Norman/DeWitt, Robin and Patricia
The Peach Tree

Pinkney, Brian
Max Found Two Sticks
Pittman, Helena Clare
A Dinosaur For Gerald
Pittman, Helena Clare
The Gift of the Willows
Polacco, Patricia
Appelemando's Dreams
Polacco, Patricia
Babushka's Doll
Polacco, Patricia
Boat Ride With Lillian Two Blossom
Polacco, Patricia
Chicken Sunday
Polacco, Patricia
Just Plain Fancy
Polacco, Patricia
Mrs. Katz And Tush
Polacco, Patricia
Some Birthday!
Polacco, Patricia
The Keeping Quilt
Polacco, Patricia
Meteor
Polacco, Patricia
Rechenka's Eggs
Polacco, Patricia
Uncle Vova's Tree
Pomerantz, Charlotte/Lessac,France
The Chalk Doll
Ponti, Leo
Song of the Swallows
Precek, Katharine Wilson/Cullen-Clark, Patricia
Penny in the Road
Priceman, Majorie
Friend or Frog
Provensen, Alice and Martin
Shaker Lane
Pryor, Bonnie/deGroat, Diane
Amanda and April
Pulver, Robin/Alley, R. W.
Mrs.Toggle's Zipper
Raschka, Chris

Charlie Parker Played Be Bop
Ringgold, Faith
Aunt Harriet's Underground Railroad In The Sky
Robertus,Polly M./Stevens, Janet
The Dog Who Had Kittens
Robinson, Nancy/Knight, Hilary
Ten Tall Soldiers
Roche, P. K.
Webster and Arnold Go Camping
Rogasky, Barbara/Hyman, Trina Schart
The Water of Life
Rogers, Jean
The Secret Moose
Roy, Ron/Cherry, Lynne
Big and Small - Short and Tall
Ryder, Joanne/Lopez, Judith
Dancers In The Garden
Ryder, Joanne/Rothman, Michael
Lizard in the Sun
Ryder, Joanne/Nolan, Dennis
Mockingbird Morning
Ryder, Joanne/Nolan, Dennis
Step Into the Night
Ryder, Joanne/Stock, Catherine
When The Woods Hum
Ryder, Joanne/Cherry, Lynne
Where Butterflies Grow
Rylant, Cyntha/Szilagyi, Mary
Night In The Country
Sanders, Scott Russell/Cogancherry, Helen
Warm As Wool
San Souci, Daniel
North Country Night
San Souci, Robert D./San Souci, Daniel
The Brave Little Tailor
San Souci, Robert/San Souci, Daniel
The Legend Of Scarface
Say, Allen
A River Dream
Schoenherr, John
Bear
Schotter, Roni/Sewall, Marcia

Van Allsburg, Chris
Two Bad Ants
Van de Wetering, Jan Willem
Hugh Pine
Vestly, Anne-Cath./Kessler, Leonard
Aurora and Socrates
Vincent, Gabrielle
Ernest and Celestine
Vincent, Gabrielle
Ernest and Celestine's Patch work Quilt
Vincent, Gabrielle
Feel Better, Ernest?
Vincent, Gabrielle
Where Are You Ernest and Celestine
Viorst, Judith/Cruz, Ray
Alexander and the Terrible, Horrible, No Good, Very Bad Day
Waber, Bernard
Ira Says Goodbye
Waber, Bernard
Ira Sleeps Over
Wallace, Ian
Chin Chiang and the Dragon's Dance
Waller, Barrett/Stevenson, Harvey
New Feet For Old
Ward, Lynd
The Biggest Bear
Warnock-Kinsey, Natalie and Kinsey, Helen/ Rand, Ted
The Bear That Heard Crying
Watson, Richard Jesse
Tom Thumb
Watts, Bernadette/Brothers Grimm
The Elves and the Shoemaker
Watts, Bernadette
Tattercoats
Watts, Leslie Elizabeth
The Troll of Sora
Weil, Lisl
Pandora's Box
Wells, Rosemary

Peabody
Wester, Helen
A Porcupine Named Fluffy
White, E. B./Williams, Garth
Charlotte's Web
Wild, Margaret/Huxley, Dee
Mr. Nick's Knitting
Wild, Margaret/Vivas, Julie
The Very Best of Friends
Wildsmith, Brian
A Christmas Story
Willard, Nancy/Pinkney, Jerry
A Starlit Somersault Downhill
Willard, Nancy/dePaola, Tomie
The Mountains Of Quilt
Williams, Vera B.
A Chair For My Mother
Williams, Vera B./Williams, Jennifer
Stringbean's Trip To The Shining Sea
Williams, Vera B.
Three Days On A River In A Red Canoe
Winthrop, Elizabeth/Hafner, Marylin
Katherine's Doll
Winthrop, Elizabeth/Burgess, Anne
Sloppy Kisses
Wittman, Sally/Gunder Sheimer, Karen
A Special Trade
Wood, Audrey/Wood, Don
Heckedy Peg
Wood, Jakki
Animal Parade
Wood, John Norris/Dean, Kevin
Nature Hide & Seek Jungles
Woolf, Virginia/Vivas, Julie
Nurse Lugton's Curtain
Yashima, Taro
Crow Boy
Yolen, Jane/Brown, Kathryn
Eeny, Meeny, Miney, Mole
Yolen, Jane
Greyling
Yolen, Jane
Sky Dogs

Yolen, Jane/Young, Ed
The Emperor and His Kite
Yolen, Jane/Schoenherr, John
Owl Moon
Yolen, Jane/Charlip, Remy and
Maraslis, Demetra
The Seeing Stick
Yolen, Jane/Regan, Laura
Welcome To The Green House
Yorinks, Arthur/Egielski, Richard
Hey, Al
Yoshi
Who's Hiding Here
Yoshida, Toshi
Elephant Crossing
Young, Ed
Lon Po Po
Zelinsky, Paul O.
Rumpelstiltskin
Zolotow, Charlotte/Stevenson, James
I Know A Lady
Zolotow, Charlotte/McCully, Emily
Arnold
The New Friend

Grades 3 and Up, Booklist

Library shelves are full of novels telling realistic stories of children in all manner of situations-abuse, poverty, loneliness, illness. One has only to consult the card catalog to see the broad range of titles for these topics.

Not so easy to find are the types on which we chose to place our focus: books which excite the imagination through fantasy and adventure, or broaden the mind with portrayals of times past and lands far away, or warm the heart with strong, loving relationships. These are the things for which children yearn, no matter what their real-life situation.

As with the books on all levels, these books are for reading aloud. The child might be able to read them independently, but that is not the intent of this book list. As we have stated, children vary in sensitivity and you should be the one selecting read-alouds for your children (read them first to determine appropriateness).

Alexander, Lloyd/Hyman, Trina Schart
The Fortune Tellers
Allen, Robert Thomas/Pastic, George
The Violin
Allan, Ted/Blake, Quentin
Willie the Squowse

Andersen, Hans Christian/Zwergen, Lisbeth
The Swineherd
Anno, Mitsumasa
All In a Day
Anno, Mitsumasa
Anno's Aesop
Anno, Mitsumasa
Anno's Britain
Anno, Mitsumasa
Anno's Counting House
Anno, Mitsumasa
Anno's Italy
Anno, Mitsumasa
Anno's Journey
Anno, Mitsumasa
In Shadowland
Atwater, Richard & Florence/Lawson, Robert
Mr. Popper's Penguins
Babbitt, Natalie
The Search For Delicious
Baker, Olaf/Gammell, Stephen

Where The Buffaloes Begin
Bang, Molly
Dawn
Bang, Molly
Paper Crane
Base, Graeme
The Eleventh Hour
Bell, Anthea/Iwasaki, Chihiro
Swan Lake
Blume, Judy/Lisker, Sonia O.
Freckle Juice
Blume, Judy
Super Fudge
Blume, Judy/Doty, Roy
Tales Of A Fourth Grade Nothing
Bond,Michael/Forthum, Peggy
A Bear Called Paddington
Brinckloe, Julie
Fireflies
Bulla, Clyde Robert/Coalson, Glo
Dexter
Bulla, Clyde Robert/Watson, Wendy
Open The Door and See All The People
Bulla, Clyde Robert/Grant, Leigh
Shoeshine Girl
Bulla, Clyde Robert/Galdone, Paul
The Sword In The Tree
Bulla, Clyde Robert/Conover,Chris
The Wish At The Top
Bunting, Eve/Mikolaycak, Charles
The Man Who Could Call Down Owls
Burch, Robert
Ida Early Comes Over The Mountain
Burnett, Frances Hodgson/Tudor, Tasha
The Secret Garden
Burnford, Sheila/Burger, Carl
The Incredible Journey - A Tale of Three Animals
Butterworth, Oliver/Darling, Louis
The Enormous Egg

Byars, Betsy/Rogers, Jacqueline
The Blossoms Meet the Vulture Lady
Byars, Betsy/Grifalconia, Ann
The Midnight Fox
Byars,Betsy/Rogers, Jacqueline
The Not-Just-Anybody Family
Byars, Betsy
Trouble River
Carrick, Carol/Carrick, Donald
The Accident
Carrick, Carol/Carrick, Donald
The Foundling
Carrick, Carol/Carrick, Donald
Sleep Out
Carrick, Carol/Carrick, Donald
The Washout
Carrick, Donald
Harald & The Giant Knight
Carrick, Donald
Harald and the Great Stag
Caudill, Rebecca/DuBois, William Pene
A Certain Small Shepherd
Cleary, Beverly/Darling, Louis
Henry and the Clubhouse
Cleary, Beverly/Tiegreen, Alan
Ramona Forever
Cleary, Beverly/Tiegreen, Alan
Ramona Quimby, Age 8
Cleary, Beverly/Tiegreen, Alan
Ramona the Brave
Cleary, Beverly/Darling, Louis
Ramona the Pest
Coerr, Eleanor/Young, Ed
Sadako
Cohen, Barbara
The Carp in the Bathtub
Cohen, Barbara/Deraney, Michael J.
Molly's Pilgrim
Cole, Brock
The Winter Wren
Cooney, Barbara/selected by Boulton, Jane
Only Opal - (The Diary of A

Hautzig, Esther/Diamond, Donna
A Gift For Mama
Heide, Florence Parry/Gorey, Edward
The Shrinking of Treehorn
Heyer, Marilee
The Weaving of a Dream
Hodges, Margaret/Hyman, Trina Schart
Saint George and the Dragon
Holling, Holling C.
Paddle-To-The-Sea
Holmes, Efner/Tudor, Tasha
Amy's Goose
Hurwitz, Johanna/Wallner, John
Aldo Applesauce
Hurwitz, Johanna/Wallner, John
Aldo Ice Cream
Hurwitz, Johanna/Cruz, Ray
Baseball Fever
Hurwitz, Johanna/Carrick, Donald
Yellow Blue-Jay
Hutchins, Hazel/Tennent, Julie
The Three and Many Wishes of Jason Reid
Kha, Dang Manh (told by); Clark, Ann Nolan (told to)/Chen, Tony
In the Land of Small Dragon
Kind-Smith, Dick
Ace
King-Smith,Dick/Rayner, Mary
Babe the Gallant Pig
King-Smith, Dick/Rayner, Mary
Magnus Power Mouse
King-Smith, Dick/Rayner, Mary
Pigs Might Fly
Kinsey-Warrock, Natalie/Graham, Mark
Wilderness Cat
Kirk, Barbara
Grandpa, Me and Our House In The Tree
Kotzwinkle, William/Servello, Joe
Hearts of Wood and Other Timeless Tales
Lattig, Laura/Meier, David Scott
Dreamsong

Lewis, C. S./Baynes, Pauline
The Lion, the Witch and the Wardrobe
Lindgren, Astrid/Glanzman, Louis S.
Pippi Longstocking
Locke, Mary
The Summer The Spies Moved In
Locker, Thomas
The Land Of The Gray Wolf
London, Jack/Tsugami, Kyuzo
The Call Of The Wild and Other Stories
Lord, Bette Bao/Simont, Marc
In The Year Of The Boar and Jackie Robinson
Lunn, Janet/Gal, Laszlo
The Twelve Dancing Princesses
Macaulay, David
Why the Chicken Crossed the Road
MacLachlan, Patricia/Bloom, Lloyd
Arthur, For The Very First Time
MacLachlan, Patricia
Sarah, Plain and Tall
Mathis, Sharon/Dillon, Leo and Diane
The Hundred Penny Box
Mattingley, Christobel/Lacis, Astra
The Angel With A Mouth Organ
Mayer, Marianna/Mayer, Mercer
Beauty and the Beast
Mayer, Marianna/Thamer, Katie
The Black Horse
Mayer, Marianna/Hague, Michael
The Unicorn and the Lake
Mayer, Mercer
East Of The Sun and West Of The Moon
Mayer, Mercer
The Sleeping Beauty (retold)
Mayne, William/Stubley, Trevor
The Yellow Airplane
McCloskey, Robert

Homer Price
McKissack, Patricia C./Isadora, Rachel
Flossie and the Fox
Mikolaycak, Charles
Babushka
Miles, Miska/Parnall, Peter
Annie and the Old One
Moeri, Louise/Hyman, Trina Schart
Star Mother's Youngest Child
Moeri, Louise/Goode,Diane
Unicorn and Plow
Mukerji, Dhan Gopal
Gay-Neck
Murphy, Shirley Rousseau/Sibley, Don
The Flight of the Fox
Ness, Evaline
Sam, Bangs and Moonshine
Nixon,Joan Lowery/Cauley, Lorinda Bryan
If You Say So, Claude
Nixon,Joan Lowery/Pearson, Tracey Campbell
Fat Chance, Claude
Nixon, Joan Lowery/Pearson, Tracey Campbell
You Bet Your Britches, Claude
North, Sterling/Schoenherr, John
Rascal
O'Brien, Robert C./Bernstein, Zena
Mrs. Frisby & the Rats of NIMH
O'Brien,Edna/Foreman, Michael
Tales For The Telling
O'Connell, Jean S./Blegvad, Erik
The Dollhouse Caper
Paterson, Katherine/Dillon, Leo and Diane
The Tale of the Mandarin Ducks
Peet, Bill
Cowardly Clyde
Polacco, Patrica
Babushka Baba Yaga
Poraziniska, Janina/Brett, Jan
The Enchanted Book

Rawlings, Marjorie Kinnan/Wyeth,N.C.
The Yearling
Rawls, Wilson
Where The Red Fern Grows
Ringgold, Faith
Dinner At Aunt Connie's House
Robinson, Barbara
The Best Christmas Pageant Ever
Rumsey, Marian/Rosier, Lydia
Beaver of Weeping Water
Rylant, Cynthia/DiGrazia, Thomas
Miss Maggie
Rylant, Cynthia/Gammell, Stephen
The Relatives Came
Rylant, Cynthia/Goode, Diane
When I Was Young In the Mountains
Sachs, Marilyn/Knight, Hilary
Matt's Mitt
San Souci, Robert D./Pinkney, Jerry
The Talking Eggs
Say, Allen
Grandfather's Jounrey
Scott, Sally
The Magic Horse
Se chan, Edmond
The String Bean
Shub, Elizabeth/Isadora, Rachel
Cutlass In The Snow
Small, David
Paper John
Speare, Elizabeth George
Sign of the Beaver
Sperry, Armstrong
Call It Courage
Spier, Peter
People
Spinelli, Jerry
Maniac Magee
Spyri, Johanna/Cheng, Judith
Heidi
Steig, William
Abel's Island

Steig, William
  Dominic
Steig, William
  The Real Thief
Steig, William
  Solomon the Rusty Nail
Steptoe, John
  Mufaro's Beautiful Daughters
Stevenson, Robert Louis/Irwin, Don
  Treasure Island
Stolz, Mary/Johnson, Pamela
  The Cuckoo Clock
Taylor, Sidney/John, Helen
  All-Of-A-Kind Family
Thompson, Colin
  The Paper Bag Prince
Titus, Eve/Galdone, Paul
  Basil of Baker Street
Tolkien, J. R. R.
  The Hobbit
Turner, Ann/Himler, Ronald
  Nettie's Trip South
Van Allsburg, Chris
  The Wreck of the Zephyr
Wallace, Bill
  Dog Called Kitty
Ward, Lynd
  The Silver Pony
Weir, Bob and Wendy/Weir, Wendy
  Panther Dream
White, E. B./Frascino, Edward
  The Trumpet of the Swan
Wilde, Oscar/Zwerger, Lisbeth
  The Selfish Giant
Wilder, Laura Ingalls/Williams, Garth
  Little House On The Prairie
Williams, Vera B.
  Scooter
Winter, Jeanette
  Follow The Drinking Gourd
Winthrop, Elizabeth/Mikolycak, Charles
  Journey To The Bright King-dom
Winthrop, Elizabeth/Hyman, Trina

Schart
  The Castle In The Attic
Zhitkov, Boris/Zelinsky, Paul O.
  How I Hunted The Little Fellows
Ziefert, Harriet/Lobel, Anita
  A New Coat For Anna

POETRY FOR YOUNGER CHILDREN

Brown, Ruth K
  Ladybug, Ladybug
Carlstrom, Nancy White/Degen, Bruce
  Better Not Get Wet, Jesse Bear
Carlstrom, Nancy White/Sandford, John
  Graham Cracker Animals 1-2-3
Carlstrom, Nancy White/Degen, Bruce
  It's About Time, Jesse Bear and Other Rhymes
Carlstrom, NancyWhite/Pinkney,Jerry
  Wild Wild Sunflower Child Anna
Clark, Emma Chichester
  I Never Saw A Purple Cow and Other Nonsense Rhymes
Coleridge, Sara/Oliver, Jenni
  January Bring the Snow
Dragonwagon, Crescent/Pinkney, Jerry
  Half A Moon and One Whole Star
Guarino, Deborah/Kellogg, Steven
  Is Your Mama A Llama?
Hague, Kathleen/Hague, Michael
  Bear Hugs
Henderson, Kathy/Thompson, Carol
  Bounce Bounce Bounce
Henderson, Kathy/Thompson, Carol
  Bumpety Bump
Lear, Edward/Brett, Jan
  The Owl and the Pussycat

Martin, Bill Jr. and Archambault, John/ Rand, Ted
Barn Dance!
Marzollo, Jean/Pinkney, Jerry
Pretend You're A Cat
McMillan, Bruce
One Sun
Merriam Eve/Wilhelm, Hans
Blackberry Ink
Pomerantz, Charlotte/Tafuri, Nancy
All Asleep
Prelutsky, Jack (selected by)/Brown, Marc
Read-Aloud Rhymes tor the Very Young

POETRY FOR OLDER CHILDREN

Demi
Demi's Secret Garden
Demi (selected and illustrated by)/Huang, Tze-Si (translated by)
In the Eyes of the Cat - Japanese Poetry for All Seasons
Frank, Josette (Nature Poems selected by)/Locker, Thomas (Painting by)
Snow Toward Evening-A Year in a River Valley
Frost, Robert/Young, Ed
Birches
Greenfield, Eloise/Dillon, Diane and Leo
Honey, I Love and Other Love Poems
Greenfield, Eloise/Gilchrist, Jan Spivey
Nathaniel Talking
Greenfield, Eloise/Ferguson, Amos Mr.
Under the Sunday Tree
Grimes, Nikki/Cooper, Floyd
Meet Danita Brown
Hirschi, Ron/Mangelsen, Thomas D. (color photographs by)
Spring
Hirschi, Ron/Mangelsen, Thomas D.

(color photographs by)
Winter
Holman, Felice/Spanfeller, Jim
King-Smith, Dick (selected by)/Wild, Jocelyn
The Animal Parade
Jeffers, Susan (Paintings By)
Brother Eagle, Sister Sky
Little Lessie Jones/Gilchrist, Jan Spivey
Children of Long Ago
Livingston, Myra Cohn (Poet)/Fisher, Leonard, Everett (Painter)
Celebrations
Livingston, Myra Cohn (poet)/Fisher, Leonard, Everett (painter)
Sea Songs
Livingston, Myra Cohn/Fisher, Leonard,Everett
Sky Songs
Longfellow, Henry Wadsworth/Jeffers, Susan
Hiawatha
Longfellow, Henry Wadsworth/Rand, Ted
Paul Revere s Ride
Myers, Walter Dean
Brown Angels
Siebert, Diane/Minor, Wendell (paintings by)
Heartland
Siebert, Diane/Minor, Wendell (paintings by)
Mojave
Siebert, Diane/Minor,Wendell
Sierra
Siebert, Diane/Minor, Wendell
Train Song
Sullivan, Charles (edited by)
Imaginary Gardens- American
Poetry and Art for Young People
Yolen Jane/Lewin, Ted
Bird Watch

POETRY FOR ALL AGES

Adoff Arnold and Pinkney, Jerry
In For Winter, Out For Spring
Carle, Eric
Eric Carle's Animals Animals
Field, Eugene/Street, Janet
The Gingham Dog and the Calico Cat
Hopkins, Lee Bennett/Milone, Karen
Still As A Star
Kitchen, Bert
Gorilla/Chinchilla
Larrick, Nancy (poems compiled by)/
Young, Ed (drawings)
Cats Are Cats
Larrick, Nancy (poems complied by)
Young, Ed (drawings)
Mice Are Nice
Lewis, Patrick/Chess, Victoria
A Hippopotamusn't
Livingston, Myra Cohn (selected by)
Hyman, Trina Schart
Cat Poems
Martin, Bill Jr. and Archambault, John/
Endicott, James
Listen to the Rain
O'Neill, Mary/Wallner, John
Hailstones and Halibut Bones
Royds, Caroline (complied by)
Poems for Young Children
Ryder Joanne/NoCan, Dennis
Under Your Feet
San Souci, Daniel
North Country Night
Stevenson, Robert Louis/Edens,
Cooper (conceived and collected by)
A Child's Garden of Verses
Stevenson, Robert Louis/Hague,
Michael
The Land of Nod

The Emergent Reader

Once children learn how to read, they need <u>quantities</u> of books to help them instantly recognize vocabulary and promote fluency. Providing the best books at this stage to help children become "absorbed" readers (reading as primary choice of recreation) is vital. Finding picture books or "series" books (books with a vocabulary written specifically for the young reader) becomes the greatest challenge.

Matching a child's reading vocabulary with books in the library and bookstore can be a dilemma for *all* of us working with young readers. It can be very time consuming and, at times, confusing. We suggest the following tips that may lessen the stress of finding appropriate reading material.

• Try to match school reading vocabulary with library books.
• Find a suggested list of books for beginning readers and compare the vocabulary with your child's reading program.
• Know "reading series" and publishers that focus on books for the beginning reader.

By familiarizing yourself with the various series, you will be able to decide which books are appropriate for your child. Your public library or bookstore will be happy to help you locate the following series:

A Giant First-Start Reader	Troll Associates
A Golden Easy Reader	Western Publishing Company
A Golden Look-Look Book	Western Publishing Company
A Golden Very Easy Reader	Western Publishing Company
A Just One More Book Just For You	Children's Press
A Random House Pictureback Reader	Random House
A Rookie Reader	Children's Press
A Stickerbook Reader	Harper Collins Publishers
All Aboard Books	Grosset and Dunlap
All Aboard Reading	Grosset and Dunlap
An Early I Can Read Book	Harper and Row Publishers
An I Can Read Book	Harper Trophy Publishers
Bank Street Ready-to-Read	Bantam Doubleday Dell Publishing Group
Dial-Easy-to-Read	Dial Books for Young Readers
Discovery Readers	Ideals Children's Books
Get Ready-Get Set Read	Barron's
Hello Reading	Penquin Books USA, Inc.
Hello Reader	Scholastic, Inc.
Milliken's Children's Classics	Milliken's Publishing Company
My First Reader	Children's Press
Puffin Easy-to-Read	Penquin Books USA, Inc.
Reading Programme	Ladybird Books
Reading Well	Milliken Publishing Company
Real Reading	Steck Vaughn Company
Sesame Street Start-to-Read	Random House Children's Television Workshop
School Zone Start-To-Read	School Zone Publishing Company
Start-Off-Stories	Random House
Step-Into-Reading	Random House

Beginning Reader Booklist

Many of the books on our list were written specifically for the beginning reader and are usually part of a series of books such as the **Step-into-Reading Series** published by Random House or the **I Can Read Series** published by Harper & Row.

Other books on the list are picture books written, not specifically for the beginning reader, but rather for pleasure, and while they do not contain a predetermined vocabulary, many, we've found, work equally well for the beginning reader. We have made every effort to place these in appropriate levels, but you may find a few words that your child will need help with.

This list of books progresses steadily from level to level; books in one level are slightly more difficult than those in the preceding level. Books in **Level 1** have only a few words. These words can be easily remembered after one reading. The child can look at the pictures to find clues for most of the words.

Books in **Level 2** continue to have a minimum number of words and lots of repetition. Many of the words can be sounded out (such as words with beginning consonant sounds and short vowels such as run, rat, mud). Stories continue to have picture clues but may also have repeating sentence patterns (cat knocked over the lamp, dog knocked over the lamp, mouse knocked over the lamp). Many of the stories are the words to familiar songs and rhymes.

Books in **Level 3** actually engage the children in reading. They are now utilizing the reading skills learned in school (blending sounds, thinking about how the word sounds within the sentence and looking to the illustrations for clues). The text of the story becomes slightly longer and words that can only be recognized by sight (Dolch words such as were, was, there etc.) are introduced.

Books in **Levels 4 - 8** progress in difficulty introducing more words and longer text. While children are reading books in these levels, they are working hard to become fluent (reading words together whereas before they were reading word by word). This is the result of internalizing reading skills as well as many, many hours of practice time. Ultimately, by the end of **Level 8**, your child will be reading smoothly and using expression as he/she reads.

TIPS FOR PARENTS OF BEGINNING READERS

1. The books in this list will be used by children to practice reading skills. It is important for an adult to be sitting close by to help with unfamiliar words and to offer praise and encouragement.

2. Drop back a level if the child appears frustrated.

3. Some books have a lot more words on a page than other books within the same level. They were included because the text was very repetitive.

4. Your child may stay on some levels for a very long time, but progress through others quite quickly. This is normal.

5. It is fun for children to see how far they have come with their reading. Dropping back a level and breezing through those books gives them a good feeling.

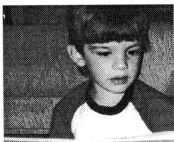

BEGINNING READER BOOKLIST—LEVEL 1

Anholt, Catherine
   Good Days Bad Days
Burton, Marilee Robin
   Tail Toes Eyes Ears Nose
Carle, Eric
   Have You Seen My Cat?
Charles, Donald
   Calico Cat Looks At Colors
Coxe, Molly
   Whose Footprints?
Ehlert, Lois
   Color Zoo
Ernst, Lisa Campbell/Ernst, Lee
   The Bee
Ernst, Lisa Campbell
   Up To Ten And Down Again
Gomi, Taro
   Who Ate It?
Gomi, Taro
   Who Hid It?
Gomi,Taro
   Where's The Fish?
Hubbard, Woodleigh
   2 Is For Dancing
Karlin, Bernie
   Meow

Koffman, Phyllis/Wilson,Sarah
   We Play
McMillan, Bruce
   Play Day
Maestro, Betsy and Giulio
   Camping Out - A Book of Action Words
Maestro, Betsy and Giulio
   On The Go - A Book of Adjectives
McMillan, Bruce
   Here A Chick, There A Chick
McMillan, Bruce
   One Sun - A Book of Terse Verse
Miller, Margaret
   Whose Shoe?
Moncure, Jane Belk/ Hohag, Linda Sommers
   Hi, Word Bird!
Paterson, Bettina
   My First Wild Animal
Pirotta, Saviour/Butler, Stephen
   Little Bird
Shapiro, Arnold L./Wellington, Monica
   Who Says That?
Stott, Dorothy
   Little Duck's Bicycle Ride
Tafuri, Nancy
   Do Not Disturb
Tafuri, Nancy
   Early Morning In The Barn
Tafuri, Nancy
   Have You Seen My Duckling?
Tafuri, Nancy
   Rabbit's Morning
Tafuri, Nancy
   Who's Counting?
Tester, Sylvia Root/Hauge, Carl and Mary
   Chase!
Wildsmith, Brian
   Brian Wildsmith's ABC
Yektai, Niki/Brewster, Patience
   Sun Rain

BEGINNING READER BOOKLIST—LEVEL 2

Aruego, Jose and Dewey, Ariane
We Hide, You Seek
Beck, Jan
Five Little Ducks
Brown, Craig
My Barn
Christensen, Nancy/Hockerman, Dennis
Good Night, Little Kitten
Corey, Dorothy/Axeman, Lois
You Go Away
de Regniers, Beatrice Schenk
Going For A Walk
Fehlner, Paul/Chambliss, Maxie
Dog and Cat
Florian, Douglas
At The Zoo
Hague, Michael (illustrated by)
Teddy Bear Teddy Bear
Halpern, Shari
My River
Gerstein, Mordicai
Roll Over!
Greene, Carol/Sharp, Gene
Please Wind?
Greene, Carol/Fredrick, Larry
Rain! Rain!
Hamsa, Bobbie/Sharp, Paul
Dirty Larry
Hamsa, Bobbie/Warshaw, Jerry
Polly Wants A Cracker
Hillert, Margaret/Anderson, Irv
The Little Runaway
Jensen, Patricia/Delaney, Molly
The Mess
Kingsley, Perl/Brown, Richard
I Can Do It Myself
Levinson, Ricki/Kelley, True
Touch! Touch!
Lewison, Wendy Cheyette/Cocca-Leffler, Maryann
Mud
Martin, Bill Jr./Carle, Eric

Brown Bear, Brown Bear What Do You See?
Matthias, Catherine/Neill, Eileen Mueller
Out The Door
McKissack, Patricia and Fredrick/Dunnington, Tom
Cinderella
McKissack, Patricia and Fredrick/Hockerman, Dennis
The Little Red Hen
McKissack, Patricia C./Martin, Clovis
Who Is Coming?
Milos, Rita/Martin, Clovis
I Am
Namm, Diane/McCue, Lisa
Little Bear
Namm, Diane/Chambliss, Maxie
Monsters
Packard, Mary/Huang, Benrei
The Kite
Packard, Mary/Huang, Benrei
Surprise
Petrie, Catherine/Warshaw, Jerry
Joshua James Likes Trucks
Sampton, Sheila White
Moon To Sun An Adding Book
Sampton, Sheila White
On The River An Adding Book
Spier, Peter
Fast-Slow High-Low - A Book of Opposites
Tafuri, Nancy
Spots, Feathers, and Curly Tails
Thaler, Mike/Smath, Jerry
Seven Little Hippos
Thaler, Mike/Grossman, Robert
What Could A Hippopotamus Be?
Upton, Pat/Novak, Matt
Who Does This Job?
Upton, Pat/Schmidt, Karen Lee
Who Lives In The Woods?
Williams, Sue/Vivas, Julie

I Went Walking
Wylie, Joanne and David
A Funny Fish Story
Yektai, Niki/deGroat, Diane
Bears In Pairs
Yektai, Niki/Ryan, Susannah
What's Missing
Zinnemann-Hope, Pam/Denton, Kady
MacDonald
Let's Go Shopping, Ned
Zinnemann-Hope, Pam/Denton, Kady
MacDonald
Let's Play Ball, Ned
Zinnemann-Hope, Pam/Denton, Kady
MacDonald
Time For Bed, Ned

BEGINNING READER BOOKLIST— LEVEL 3

Adams, Phylliss; Hartson, Eleanor;
Taylor, Mark/Hockerman, Dennis
Hi! Dog
Aruego, Jose and Dewey, Ariane
(illustrated by)
Five Little Ducks - Raffi Songs to Read
Blackstone, Margaret/O'Brien, John
This Is Baseball
Burningham, John
The School
Burningham, John
The Snow
Christelow, Eileen (retold)
Five Little Monkeys Jumping On The Bed
Cohen, Caron Lee/Karas, G. Brian
Pigeon, Pigeon
Dabcovich, Lydia
Sleepy Bear
Farjeon, Eleanor/Jenkins, Mary Price
Cats Sleep Anywhere
Foster, Kelli C. and Erickson, Gina C./
Gifford, Kerri
Find Nat
Foster, Kelli C. and Erickson, Gina C./

Gifford, Kerri
Pip And Kip
Foster, Kelli C. and Erickson, Gina C./
Gifford, Kerri
The Sled Surprise
Fox, Mem/Mullins, Patricia
Hattie and the Fox
Frankel, Julie E./Martin, Clovis
Oh No, Otis!
Galdone, Paul
Cat Goes Fiddle-i-fee
Griest, Virginia/Wellington, Monica
In Between
Hamsa, Bobbie/Hayes, Stephen
Fast Draw Freddie
Hillert, Margaret/Masheris, Robert
Away Go The Boats
Hillert, Margaret/Sumichrast
The Funny Ride
Hillert, Margaret/Martin, Dick
Play Ball
Hillert, Margaret/Stasisk, Krystyna
The Purple Pussycat
Hillert, Margaret/Hockerman, Dennis
Tom Thumb
Hillert, Margaret/Brooks, Nan
Who Goes To School?
Jensen, Patricia/Becker, Wayne
My House
Langstaff, John/Parker, Nancy Winslow
Oh, A-Hunting We Will Go
Lawson, Carol
Teddy Bear, Teddy Bear
Lillegard, Dee/Agee, Jon
Sitting In My Box
Lockwood, Primrose/Vulliamy, Clara
Cat Boy!
Manson, Christopher
A Farmyard Song
Maris, Ron
Are You There, Bear?
McKissack, Patricia and Fredrick/
Martin, Clovis
Bugs!
Minarik, Else Holmelund/Graham,

Margaret Bloy
It's Spring!
Mueller, Virginia/Munsinger, Lynn
Monster and the Baby
Packard, David/Alley, Robert W.
The Ball Game
Paterson, Diane
Soap and Suds
Petrie, Catherine/Elzaurdia, Sharon
Sandbox Betty
Reese, Bob and Nancy/Reese, Bob
Sack Lunch
Ruane, Joanna/Boyd, Patti
Boats, Boats, Boats
Shelby, Anne/Trivas, Irene
What To Do About Polution
Stadler, John
Cat Is Back At Bat
Watanabe, Shigeo/Ohtomo, Yasuo
Get Set! Go!
Watanabe, Shigeo/Ohtomo, Yasuo
How Do I Put It On?
Watanabe, Shigeo/Ohtomo, Yasuo
I Can Ride It!
West, Colin
Have You Seen the Crocodile?
West, Colin
"Hello Great Big Bullfrog!"
Westcott, Nadine Bernard
Skip To My Lou
Wheeler, Cindy
Marmalade's Nap
Yektai, Niki/Ryan, Susannah
What's Silly?
Ziefert, Harriet and Ray, Deborah
Kogan
**New Boots For Spring - A
Book of Seasons**
Ziefert, Harriet/Baruffi, Andrea
The Wheels On The Bus
Zinnemann-Hope, Pam/Denton, Kady
MacDonald
Find Your Coat, Ned

**BEGINNING READER
BOOKLIST—LEVEL 4**
Adams, Phylliss; Hartson, Eleanore;
Taylor,   Mark/Sandford, John
Stop the Bed!
Bridgman, Elizabeth
New Dog Next Door
Brown, Marc
Pickle Things
Burningham, John
The Baby
Burningham, John
The Rabbit
Butterworth, Nick/Inkpen, Mick
Jasper's Beanstalk
Bvivin, Kelly/Martin, Clovis
Where Is Mittens?
Casey, Patricia
Quack Quack
Charles, Donald
Calico Cat At School
Charles, Donald
Fat, Fat, Calico Cat
Corey, Dorothy/Axeman, Lois
Everyone Takes Turns
Dabcovich, Lydia
Ducks Fly
Dale, Penny
Bet You Can't
Dale, Penny
The Elephant Tree
Dale, Penny
Wake Up, Mr. B.!
Eastman, P. D.
Are You My Mother?
Florian, Douglas
A Carpenter
Florian, Douglas
Turtle Day
Foster, Kelli C. and Erickson, Gina C./
Gifford, Kerri
A Mop For Pop
Foster, Kelli C. and Erickson, Gina C./
Gifford, Kerri
Bat's Surprise

Foster, Kelli C. and Erickson, Gina C./
Gifford, Kerri
Jake And The Snake
Foster, Kelli C. and Erickson, Gina C./
Gifford, Kerri
Sometimes I Wish
Foster, Kelli C. and Erickson, Gina C./
Gifford, Kerri
The Bug Club
Foster, Kelli C. and Erickson, Gina C./
Gifford, Kerri
What A Day For Flying
Foster, Kelli C. and Erickson, Gina C./
Gifford, Kerri
Whiptail Of Blackshale Trail
Galdone, Paul
Three Little Kittens
Ginsburg, Mirra/Tafuri, Nancy
Across the Stream
Gordan, Sharon/Page, Don
Drip, Drop
Gordan, Sharon/Page, Don
Play Ball, Kate
Henley, Claire
Farm Day
Herman, Gail/Gorbaty, Norman
**Time for School Little Dino-
saur**
Hillert, Margaret/Axeman, Lois
I Like Things
Iwamura, Kazuo
Tan Tan's Hat
Javernick, Ellen/Hackney, Rick
Where's Brooke?
Kandoian, Ellen
Maybe She Forgot
Kessler, Ethel and Leonard/ Paris, Pat
Pig's New Hat
Lloyd, David/Voake, Charlotte
Duck
Lunn, Carolyn/Dunnington, Tom
Bobby's Zoo
Lunn, Carolyn/Martin, Clovis
A Whisper Is Quiet
Martin, Bill Jr.and Archambault, John/

Rand, Ted
Here Are My Hands
Matthias, Catherine/Sharp, Gene
Over-Under
Matthias,Catherine/Sharp, Gene
Too Many Balloons
Mayer, Mercer
Little Critter's The Picnic
Mayer, Mercer
**Little Critter's These Are My
Pets**
Mayer, Mercer
This Is My Friend
McKissack, Patricia and Fredrick/Bala,
Virginia
The Three Bears
McKissack, Patricia and Fredrick/
Dunnington,   Tom
Three Billy Goats Gruff
McMillan, Bruce
Kitten Can . . .
Milios, Rita/Ching
The Hungry Billy Goat
Moss, Marissa
Want To Play?
Mueller, Virginia/Munsinger, Lynn
Monster Goes To School
Novak, Matt
Rolling
Ormerod, Jan
Come Back, Kittens
Ormerod, Jan
Come Back, Puppies
Otto, Carolyn/Hurd, Thacher
Dinosaur Chase
Peters, Sharon/Sims, Deborah
Five Little Kittens
Phillips, Joan/Miller, J. P.
Lucky Bear
Pizer, Abigail
It's A Perfect Day
Radlauer, Ruth Shaw/McCully, Emily
Arnold
Breakfast By Molly
Robart, Rose/Kovalski, Maryann

The Cake That Mack Ate
Rosen, Michael/Oxenbury, Helen
   We're Going On A Bear Hunt
Ross, Katharine/Cooke, Tom
   Grover, Grover, Come On Over
Scarry, Richard
   Richard Scarry's Watch Your Step, Mr. Rabbit
Serfozo, Mary/Narahashi, Keiko
   Who Said Red?
Stanley, Diane (illustrated by)
   Fiddle-I-Dee
Stevens, Philippa J./Martin, Clovis
   Bonk! Goes The Ball
Testa, Fulvio
   If You Take A Paintbrush - A Book Of Colors
Thompson, Carol
   In My Bathroom
Watanabe, Shigeo/Ohtomo, Yasuo
   I Can Build A House!
Watanabe, Shigeo/Ohtomo, Yasuo
   I'm The King Of The Castle!
Westcott, Nadine Bernard
   The Lady With The Alligator Purse
Wheeler, Cindy
   Marmalade's Picnic
Wheeler, Cindy
   Marmalade's Snowy Day
Wheeler, Cindy
   Marmalade's Yellow Leaf
Wylie, Joanne and David
   Do You Know Where Your Monster Is Tonight?
Yektai, Niki/deGroat, Diane
   Hi Bears, Bye Bears
Zemach, Margot
   Hush Little Baby
Ziefert, Harriet/Stevens, Larry
   Clown Games
Ziefert, Harriet/Alley. R. W.
   The Prince Has A Boo-Boo!
Ziefert, Harriet/Siracusa, Catherine

   Say Good Night!

BEGINNING READER BOOKLIST — LEVEL 5
Adams, Phylliss; Hartson, Eleanore; Taylor, Mark/Sandford, John
   Good Show
Adams, Phylliss; Hartson, Eleanore; Taylor, Mark/Sandford, John
   Time Out!
Adams, Phylliss; Hartson, Eleanore; Taylor, Mark/Sandford, John
   Where Is Here?
Adler, David A./Cruz, Ray
   You Think It's Fun To Be A Clown!
Adorjan, Carol/Nerlove, Miriam
   I Can! Can You?
Alexander, Sue/Karas, Brian G.
   Who Goes Out On Halloween?
Anello, Christine/Thompson, Sharon
   The Farmyard Cat
Auster, Benjamin/Winborn, Marsha
   I Like It When
Awdry, Rev. W./Bell, Owain
   Happy Birthday, Thomas
Bennett, Jill (retold)/dePaola, Tomie
   Teeny Tiny
Blocksma, Mary/Kalthoff, Sandra Cox
   Rub-A-Dub-Dub - What's In The Tub
Blocksma, Mary/Kalthoff, Sandra Cox
   Where's That Duck?
Bonsall, Crosby
   And I Mean It Stanley
Borden, Louise/Hoban, Lillian
   Caps, Hats, Socks, and Mittens - A Book About the Four Seasons
Breslow, Susan and Blakemore, Sally/ Kelley, True
   I Really Want A Dog
Browne, Anthony
   Bear Hunt
Carle, Eric

The Very Hungry Caterpillar
Chalmers, Mary
Throw a Kiss, Harry
Charles, Donald
Calico Cat's Year
Coulter, Norman/Brown, Rick
Uncle Chuck's Truck
de Brunhoff, Laurent
Babar's Little Circus Star
Dodd, Lynley
A Dragon In A Wagon
Dodds, Siobhan
Charles Tiger
Dodds, Siobhan
Elizabeth Hen
Dubowski, Cathy East and Dubowski, Mark
Cave Boy
Ehrlich, Fred/Gradisher, Martha
A Class Play With Ms. Vanilla
Feldman, Eve/Banek, Yvette
Get Set and Go
Fine, Jane/Morgan, Mary
Surprise!
Gackenbach, Dick
A Bag Full Of Pups
Gachenbach, Dick
Claude and Pepper
Galdone, Paul
The Greedy Old Fat Man
Gerstein, Mordicai
Follow Me!
Goennel, Heidi
My Dog
Hamm, Diane Johnston/Palmer, Kate Salley
How Many Feet In The Bed?
Hamm, Diane Johnston/Brown, Rick
Rock-A-Bye Farm
Harrison, David L./Wilhelm, Hans
Wake Up, Sun!
Hawkins, Colin and Jacqui
Jen the Hen
Hayward, Linda/Munsinger, Lynn
Hello, House!

Hill, Eric
Spot In The Garden
Hill, Eric
Spot Looks At Colors
Hill, Eric
Spot's First Christmas
Hill, ERic
Where's Spot?
Hooks, William/Baseman, Gary
A Dozen Dizzy Dogs
Iwamura, Kazuo
Tan Tan's Suspenders
Iwamura, Kazuo
Ton and Pon - Big and Little
Jonas, Ann
Two Bear Cubs
Jonas,Ann
When You Were A Baby
Kovalski, Maryann (An adaptation)
The Wheels On The Bus
Kraus, Robert/Aruego, Jose
Whose Mouse Are You?
Landstrom, Olof and Lena/Dyssegaard, Elisabeth (translated by)
Will Gets A Haircut
Lerner, Sharon/Mathieu, Joe
Big Bird's Copycat Day
Levine, Abby/Apple, Margot
You Push, I Ride
London, Jonathan/Remkiewicz, Frank
Froggy Gets Dressed
Long, Earlene/Brown, Richard
Gone Fishing
Mason, Margo/Gottlieb, Dale
Are We There Yet?
Mason, Margo/Siracusa,Catherine
Ready, Alice?
Matthias, Catherine/Dunnington, Tom
I Love Cats
Mayer, Mercer
Little Critter's Little Sister's Birthday
Mayer, Mercer
Little Critter's Staying Over-night

Mayer, Mercer
  Little Critter's This Is My House
McDaniel, Becky Bring/Axeman, Lois
  Katie Couldn't
McKissack, Patricia and Fredrick/ Sikorski, Anne
  Country Mouse and City Mouse
McKissack, Patricia and Fredrick/ Anderson, Peggy Perry
  The Frog Prince
McKissack, Patricia and Fredrick/ Anderson, Peggy Perry
  King Midas and His Gold
McKissack, Patricia and Fredrick/ Hackney, Richard
  Messy Bessey
McKissack, Patricia and Fredrick/ Anderson, Peggy Perry
  The Ugly Little Duck
McLenighan, Valjean/McKissack, Vernon
  Turtle and Rabbit
Milos, Rita/Martin, Clovis
  Sneaky Pete
Moncure, Jane Belk/Hook, Frances
  Fall Is Here!
Moncure, Jane Belk/Hohag, Linda Sommers
  Hide-And-Seek Word Bird
Morgan, Michaela/Porter, Sue
  Edward Gets A Pet
Morris, Neil/Stevenson, Peter
  I'm Big
Moses, Amy/Hackney, Rick
  I Am An Explorer
Mueller, Virginia/Munsinger, Lynn
  Monster's Birthday Hiccups
Neasi, Barbara/Sharp, Gene
  Listen to Me
Novak, Matt
  Elmer Blunts Open House
O'Connor, Jane/Alley, R. W.
  The Teeny Tiny Woman

O'Donnell, Elizabeth Lee/Chambliss, Maxie
  I Can't Get My Turtle To Move
Oppenheim, Joanne/Schindler, S. D.
  Eency, Weency Spider
Peters, Sharon/Rosenberg, Amye
  Five Little Kittens
Peters, Sharon/Connor, Eulala
  Here Comes Jack Frost
Phillips, Joan/Gorbaty, Norman
  Tiger Is A Scaredy Cat
Phillips, Joan/Munsinger, Lynn
  My New Boy
Rogers, Paul/Corfield, Robin Bell
  Somebody's Awake
Ross, Katharine (Adapted by)/ Oberdieck, Bernhard
  The Ugly Duckling
Schade, Susan/Buller, Jon
  Railroad Toad
Seuss, Dr.
  Green Eggs and Ham
Sharp, Paul
  Paul the Pitcher
Shaw, Nancy/Apple, Margot
  Sheep In A Jeep
Silverman, Martin/Aitken, Amy
  My Tooth Is Loose
Taylor, Judy/Gantner, Susan
  Sophie and Jack
Taylor, Judy/Gantner, Susan
  Sophie and Jack Help Out
Townson, Hazel/Rees, Mary
  What On Earth?
Wang, Mary Lewis/Ching
  The Ant and The Dove (Aesop Tale Retold)
Wang, Mary Lewis/Connelly, Gwen
  The Frog Prince
Watson, Wendy
  Jamie's Story
Wheeler, Cindy
  A Good Day, A Good Night
Wheeler, Cindy
  Marmalade's Christmas

Present
Wheeler, Cindy
Rose
Yabuuchi, Masayuki
Animals Sleeping
Ziefert, Harriet/Schumacher, Claire
Cat Games
Ziefert, Harriet/Rader, Laura
Goody New Shoes
Ziefert, Harriet/Smith, Mavis
Harry Gets Ready For School
Ziefert, Harriet/Rader, Laura
I Hate Boots!
Ziefert, Harriet/Gorbaty,Norman
No More TV, Sleepy Dog
Ziefert, Harriet/Alley, R. W.
The Prince's Tooth Is Loose
Ziefert, Harriet/Gorbaty, Norman
Sleepy Dog
Ziefert, Harriet,/Aitken, Amy
Stitches
Ziefert, Harriet/Aitken, Amy
Take My Picture
Ziefert, Harriet/Childers, Argus
Wish For A Fish
Ziefert, James/Smith, Mavis
Harry Goes Camping

BEGINNING READER BOOKLIST — LEVEL 6
Adler,David A./Gackenbach, Dick
My Dog and the Green Sock Mystery
Adler, David A./Barton, Byron
My Dog and the Key Mystery
Alborough, Jez
The Grass Is Always Greener
Asch, Frank
Skyfire
Baker, Bonnie Jeanne
A Pear By Itself
Barrett, Judi/Barrett, Ron
Animals Should Definitely Not Wear Clothing

Bartholomew
My Friend Horace
Benner,Barbara/Siracusa,Catherine
Beef Stew
Berger, Barbara Helen
When the Sun Rose
Blocksma, Mary/Kalthoff, Sandra Cox
All My Toys Are On The Floor
Blocksma, Mary/Kalthoff, Sandra Cox
The Best Dressed Bear
Boegehold, Betty D./Michaut, Valerie
You Are Much Too Small
Brown, Ruth
Our Puppy's Vacation
Burningham, John
Come Away From The Water, Shirley
Burningham, John
Mr. Gumpy's Outing
Burningham, John
Seasons
Butler, Dorothy/Fuller, Elizabeth
My Brown Bear Barney
Byars, Betsy/Truesdell, Sue
The Golly Sisters Go West
Carlson, Nancy
Poor Carl
Carlstrom, Nancy White/Wickstrom, Thor
I'm Not Moving, Mama!
Cole, Joanna/Munsinger, Lynn
Norma Jean, Jumping Bean
Cole, Joanna/Hafner, Marylin
The Missing Tooth
Compton, Kenn
Happy Christmas To All!
Dabcovich, Lydia
Mrs. Huggins and Her Hen Hannah
Denton, Kady MacDonald
Janet's Horses
Edwards, Roberta/Wickstrom, Sylvie
Five Silly Fisherman
Feldman, Eve/Weissman, Bari
The Squire Takes A Wife

Frankel, Julie E./Smith, Ted
Hare and Bear
Gackenbach, Dick
Binky Gets A Car
Gackenbach, Dick
Claude the Dog
Gackenbach, Dick
Supposes
Gackenbach, Dick
What's Claude Doing?
Graham, John/dePaola, Tomie
I Love You Mouse
Greene, Carol/Boddy, Joe
Blue Ben
Greene, Carol/Martin, Clovis
Miss Apple's Hats
Halloran, Phyllis/Ching
Cat Purrs
Hayward, Linda/Chartier, Normand
All Stuck Up
Heilbroner, Joan/Murdocca, Sal
Tom the TV Cat
Henley, Claire
Jungle Day
Hennessy, B. G./Galli, Letizia
Eeny, Meeney, Miney, Mo
Hoban, Julia/Hoban, Lillian
Amy Loves the Rain
Hoban, Julia/Hoban, Lillian
Amy Loves the Snow
Hooker, Tuth/Apple, Margot
Sara Loves Her Big Brother
Hulbert, Jay/Killgrew, John
Pete Pig Cleans Up
Hutchins, Pat
**You'll Soon Grow Into Them,
Titch**
Isadora, Rachel
Max
Iwamura, Kazuo
**Ton and Pon Two Good
Friends**
Joyce, William
George Shrinks
Keats, Ezra Jack

Whistle For Willie
Keller, Holly
Geraldine's Blanket
Keller, Holly
Ten Sleepy Sheep
Kingman, Lee/Natti, Susanna
Catch the Baby!
Kraus, Robert/Aruego, Jose
Leo The Late Bloomer
Kraus, Robert/Aruego, Jose and
Dewey, Ariane
Owliver
Kwitz, Mary DeBall/Degen, Bruce
Little Chick's Friend Duckling
Lloyd, David/Voce, Louise
Hello, Goodbye
Lobel, Arnold
Small Pig
Maris, Ron
Hold Tight, Bear!
Mason, Margo/ Schumacher, Claire
Two Good Friends
McKissack, Patricia and Fredrick/
Mitter, Kathy
Tall Phil and Small Bill
McLenighan, Valjean/Hamilton, Laurie
Three Strikes and You're Out
McPhail, David
Emma's Pet
McPhail, David
Emma's Vacation
McPhail, David
Fix-It
McPhail, David
Lost!
Moncure, Jane Belk/Hook, Frances
**I Never Say I'm Thankful, But
I Am**
Morgan, Michaela/Porter, Sue
Edward Hurts HIs Knee
Most, Bernard
The Cow That Went Oink
Narahashi, Keiko
I Have A Friend
Nelson, Brenda/Brown, Richard

Mud For Sale
Noll, Sally
Watch Where You Go
Novak, Matt
Claude and Sun
Oppenheim, Joanne/Schindler, S.D.
Could It Be?
Oppenheim, Joanne/Demarest, Chris
The Donkey's Tale
Parish, Peggy/Watts, James
Good Hunting Blue Sky
Parker, Nancy Winslow
Poofy Loves Company
Rockwell, Anne/Rockwell, Lizzy
Apples and Pumpkins
Schlein, Miriam/Auclair, Joan
Big Talk
Seuss, Dr.
The Cat In The Hat
Shaw, Nancy/Apple, Margot
Sheep On A Ship
Shaw, Nancy/Apple, Margot
Sheep In A Shop
Thaler, Mike/Wiesner, David
Owly
Thompson, Carol
In My Bedroom
Tripp, Valerie/Kalthoff, Sandra Cox
Baby Koala Finds A Home
Tripp, Valerie/Martin, Sandra Kalthoff
Happy, Happy, Mother's Day!
Tripp, Valerie/Kalthoff, Sandra Cox
The Penguin's Paint
Tripp, Valerie/Martin, Sandra Kalthoff
Sillyhen's Big Surprise
Tripp, Valerie/Kalthoff, Sandra Cox
The Singing Dog
Udry, Janice May/Simont, Marc
A Tree Is Nice
Wahl, Robert/Ewers, Joe
Friend Dog
Waverly,Barney/Henry, Steve
How Big? How Fast? How Hungry? A Book About Cats
Wildsmith, Brian

Give A Dog A Bone
Wildsmith, Brian
What The Moon Saw
Winter, Jeanette
Come Out To Play
Wood, Audrey/Wood, Don
The Napping House
Yoshi
The Butterfly Hunt
Ziefert, Harriet/Prebenna, David
A Car Trip For Mole And Mouse
Ziefert, Harriet/Gundersheimer, Karen
Chocolate Mud Cake
Ziefert, Harriet/Rader, Laura
Follow Me!
Ziefert, Harriet/Baruffi, Andrea
Good Night, Everyone!
Ziefert, Harriet/Rader, Laura
Penny Goes To The Movies
Ziefert, Harriet/Nicklaus, Carol
So Hungry!
Ziefert, Harriet/Nicklaus, Carol
So Sick!

BEGINNING READER BOOKLIST — LEVEL 7
Abercrombie, Barbara/Graham, Mark
Charlie Anderson
Appleby, Ellen (pictures by)
The Three Billy Goats Gruff
Asch, Frank
Happy Birthday Moon
Asch, Frank
Bear's Bargain
Asch, Frank
Bear Shadow
Asch, Frank
Moongame
Bemelmans, Ludwig
Madeline
Benchley, Nathaniel/Lobel, Arnold
Sam the Minuteman
Berger, Barbara
Grandfather Twilight

Brandenberg, Franz/Aliki
Leo and Emily and the Dragon
Brenner, Barbara/McCully, Emily Arnold
Beavers Beware!
Brenner, Barbara/Gaban, J.
Moon Boy
Brown, Margaret Wise/Williams, Garth
Wait Till The Moon Is Full
Brown, Ruth
If At First You Do Not See
Bulla, Clyde Robert/Sandin, Joan
Daniel's Duck
Byars, Betsy/Truesdell, Sue
Hooray For The Golly Sisters!
Calhoun, Mary/Young, Ed
While I Sleep
Caraway, Jane/Smath, Jerry
One Windy Day
Carlson, Nancy
Arnie Goes To Camp
Carlstrom,Nancy White/Ormai, Stella
The Moon Came Too
Celsi, Teresa/Cushman, Doug
The Fourth Little Pig
Chapman, Mary Winslow/Ching
Why?
Cherry, Lynne
Archie, Follow Me
Cocca-Leffler, Maryann
Ice-Cold Birthday
Coerr, Eleanor/Degen, Bruce
The Josefina Story Quilt
Cole, Joanna/Munsinger, Lynn
Norma Jean, Jumping Bean
Collins, David R./Wilson, Deborah
Grandfather Woo Goes To School
Collins, David R./Wilson, Deborah G.
The Wisest Answer
Cristaldo, Kathryn/Carter, Abby
Baseball Ballerina
Cushman, Doug
Aunt Eater Loves A Mystery
Damrell, Liz/Marchesi, Stephen

With the Wind
de Brunhoff, Laurent
Babar and The Ghost
de Regniers, Beatrice Schenk/Weiss, Ellen
So Many Cats!
Dubanevich, Arlene
Pigs In Hiding
Dubowski, Cathy East and Dubowski, Mark
Pretty Good Magic
Ehlert, Lois
Planting a Rainbow
Ehrlich, Amy/Alley, R. W.
Buck-Buck the Chicken
Ericsson, Jennifer A./Eitan, Ora
No Milk!
Gammell, Stephen
Once Upon MacDonald's Farm
Garelick, May/du Bios, William Pene
Just My Size
Garland, Michael
My Cousin Katie
Gold, Porter/Karas, Brian
Who's There?
Hallinan, P. K.
We're Very Good Friends, My Father and I
Hautzig, Deborah/Brown, Marc
Happy Birthday Little Witch
Hautzig, Deborah/Brown, Marc
Little Witch's Big Night
Heiligman, Deborah/Sweet, Melissa
Into The Night
Hill, Donna/Dawson, Diane
Ms. Glee Was Waiting
Himmelman, John
Simpson Snail Sings
Hoban, Julia/Himmelman, John
Buzby
Hoff, Syd
Bernard On His Own
Holloran, Phyllis/Shoemaker, Kathryn
Oh, Brother! Oh, Sister!
Hooks, William H./Cushman, Doug

Feed Me!
Hulbert, Jay/Barnes-Murphy, Rowan
The Bedtime Beast
Hutchins, Pat
The Wind Blew
Jewell, Nancy/Thiesing, Lisa
Two Silly Trolls
Jonas, Ann
The Quilt
Joosse, Barbara M./Stock, Catherine
Better With Two
Kessler, Leonard
The Pirates' Adventure on Spooky Island
KIng, P. E./Graham, Alastair
Down On The Funny Farm
Kitamura, Satoshi
Lily Takes a Walk
Lewis, Rob
Henrietta's First Winter
Littledale,Freya/Delaney, Molly
The Farmer In The Soup
London, Jonathan/Remkiewicz, Frank
Let's Go Froggy
Lorian, Nicole/Miller, J. P.
A Birthday Present For Mama
Macdonald, Maryann/Munsinger, Lynn
Hedgehog Bakes A Cake
Macdonald, Maryann/Munsinger, Lynn
Rabbit's Birthday Kite
Mack, Jacqueline/Holloway, Jan
Tales About Tails
Magnus, Erica
Old Lars
Marshall, Edward/Marshall, James
Fox All Week
Marshall, Edward/Marshall, James
Fox At School
Marshall, Edward/Marshall, James
Fox In Love
Marshall, Edward/Marshall, James
Fox on Wheels
Marshall, James
Fox On The Job
McCully, Emily Arnold

Grandmas At Bat
McCully, Emily Arnold
Grandmas at the Lake
McCully, Emily Arnold
The Grandma Mix-Up
McKissack,Patrcia and Fredrick/Smith, Philip
No Need for Alarm
McKissack, Patricia and Fredrick/ Bartholonew
A Troll In A Hole
McPhail, David
Alligators Are Awful
McPhail, David
Andrew's Bath
McPhail, David
Sisters
McPhail, David
Those Terrible Toy-Breakers
Modell, Frank
Skeeter and the Computer
Moncure, Jane Belk/Martin, Clovis
Caring For Baby Sister
Moncure, Jane Belk/McCallum, Jodie
Caring For My Body
Moncure, Jane Belk/Rigo, Christina
Caring For My Kitty
Moncure, Jane Belk/Connelly, Gwen
Caring For My Home
Moncure, Jane Belk/Axeman, Lois
The Look Book
Moncure, Jane Belk/Hohag, Linda and Jacobson, Lori
Word Bird's Dinosaur Days
Moore, Elaine/Boddy, Joe
Mixed-Up Sam
Neuman, Pearl/Roe, Richard
When Winter Comes
O'Connor, Jane/Hamanaka, Sheila
Molly the Brave and Me
O'Connor, Jane and Robert/Lloyd, Megan
Super Cluck
Oechsli, Kelly
Mice At Bat

Otey, Mimi
Blue Moon Soup Spoon
Parish, Peggy/Tripp, Wallace
Come Back, Amelia Bedelia
Parish, Peggy/Simont, Marc
No More Monsters for Me!
Parker, Mary Jessie/Dennis, Lynne
Night Fire!
Pickett, Anola/Delaney, Ned
Old Enough for Magic
Pizer, Abigail
Loppylugs
Polette, Keith/Martin, Clovis
The Winter Duckling
Porte, Barbara Ann/Abolafia, Yossi
Harry in Trouble
Porte, Barbara Ann/Abolafia, Yossi
Harry's Dog
Porte, Barbara Ann/Abolafia, Yossi
Harry's Mom
Porte, Barbara Ann/Abolafia, Yossi
Harry's Visit
Roop, Peter and Connie/Brown, Craig
McFarland
Snips the Tinker
Rylant, Cynthia/Stevenson, Sucie
Henry and Mudge And The BedtimeThumps
Rylant, Cynthia/Stevenson, Sucie
Henry and Mudge And The Happy Cat
Rylant, Cynthia/Stevenson, Sucie
Henry and Mudge In Puddle Trouble
Rylant, Cynthia/Stevenson, Sucie
Henry and Mudge Take The Big Test
Rylant, Cynthia/Stevenson, Sucie
Henry and Mudge - The First Book
Schmidt, Karen (pictures by)
Little Red Riding Hood
Schwartz, Alvin/Weinhaus, KarenAnn
There is a Carrot in My Ear
Seguin-Fontes, Marthe

Find Me!
Shaw, Nancy/Apple, Margot
Sheep In A Shop
Singerman, Ellen/Kirchhoff, Art
Stephen's Bag
Siracusa, Catherine/Levitt, Sidney
Bingo, The Best Dog In The World
Siracusa, Catherine
No Mail For Mitchell
Smith, Mavis
A Snake Mistake
Spier, Peter
Bored - Nothing to Do!
Thaler, Mike/Chambliss, Maxie
Come And Play, Hippo
Thaler, Mike/Degen, Bruce
In the Middle of the Puddle
Tibo, Gilles
Simon and the Snowflakes
Tibo, Gilles
Simon and the Wind
Tibo, Gilles
Simon In Summer
Tibo, Gilles
Simon Welcomes Spring
Van Lann, Nancy/Westcott, Nadine Bernard
People, People Everywhere!
Van Leeuwen, Jean/Schweninger, Ann
Amanda Pig On Her Own
Van Woerkom, Dorothy O./Boddy, Joe
Tall Corn A Tall Tale
Waddell, Martin/Firth, Barbara
Can't You Sleep, Little Bear?
Wahl, Jan/Naava
My Cat Ginger
Walsh, Ellen Stoll
Mouse Count
Weir, Alison/Ray, Deborah Kogan
Peter, Good Night
Williams, Linda/Lloyd, Megan
The Little Old Lady Who Was Not Afraid of Anything
Wolff, Ashley

Come With Me
Wolkstein, Diane/Smith, Jos. A.
Step By Step

BEGINNING READER BOOKLIST — LEVEL 8

Ackerman, Karen/Gammell, Stephen
Song and Dance Man
Barracca, Debra and Sal/Buehner, Mark
The Adventures of Taxi Dog
Benchley, Nathaniel/Bolognese
George the Drummer Boy
Boegehold, Betty D./Waldman, Neil
A Horse Called Starfire
Brenner, Barbara/Boix, Manuel
The Magic Box
Brown, Marc
D. W. Thinks Big
Brown, Ruth
The Big Sneeze
Brown, Ruth
Our Cat Flossie
Burningham, John
Mr. Gumpy's Motor Car
Cameron, Ann/Strugnell,Ann
More Stories Julian Tells
Carlson, Nancy
Arnie and the New Kid
Carlson, Nancy
Harriet and the Roller Coaster
Carlson, Nancy
Harriet's Recital
Carlson, Nancy
Loudmouth George and the Big Race
Carlson, Nancy
Making the Team
Carlstrom, Nancy White/Schwartz, Amy
Blow Me a Kiss, Miss Lilly
Casely, Judith
Ada Potato
Cauley, Lorinda Bryan
The Bake-Off

Christian, Mary Blount/Dyer, Jane
Penrod Again
Christian, Mary Blount/Dyer, Jane
Penrod's Pants
Christian, Mary Blount/Schindler, S. D.
Penrod's Picture
Cole, Joanna/Wynne, Patricia
Hungry, Hungry Sharks
Cox, David
Bossyboots
dePaola, Tomie
When Everyone Was Fast Asleep
Dodd, Lynley
Hairy Maclary's Scattercat
Dodd, Lynley
Hairy Maclary's Caterwaul Caper
Dodd, Lynley
Wake Up, Bear
Dubanevich, Arlene
Pig William
Faulkner, Matt
Jack and the Beanstalk
Finsand, Mary Jane/Sandland, Reg
The Town That Moved
Gackenbach, Dick
Pepper and All The Legs
Gackenbach, Dick
The Princess and the Pea
Gackenbach,Dick
Mag the Magnificent
Galdone, Paul
The Amazing Pig
Galdone, Paul
Little Red Riding Hood
Harris, Nicholas/Horvat,Karl Josef
Owlbert
Hautzig, Deborah/Schindler, S. D.
The Pied Piper of Hamelin
Hazen, Barbara Shook/Morill, Leslie Holt
Stay, Fang
Henley, Claire
In The Ocean

Himmelman, John
The Clover Country Carrot Contest
Himmelman, John
The Day-Off Machine
Himmelman, John
The Great Leaf Blast-Off
Himmelman, John
The Super Camper Caper
Hirschi, Ron/Bash, Barbara
Forest
Hoban, Lillian
Arthur's Camp-Out
Hooks, H. William/ Meisel, Paul
Mr. Monster
Howard, Jane R.
When I'm Sleepy
Hughes, Shirley
Dogger
Jonas, Ann
The Trek
Keats, Ezra Jack
Louie's Search
Keats, Ezra Jack
Maggie and the Pirate
Keller, Holly
A Bear for Christmas
Keller, Holly
When Francie Was Sick
Keller, Holly
Will It Rain?
Krensky, Stephen/Green, Norman
Christopher Columbus
Levinson, Nancy Smiler/Sandin, Joan
Snowshoe Thompson
Littledale, Freya/Howell, Troy
Peter and the North Wind
Littledale, Freya/Seltzer, Isadore
The Twelve Dancing Princesses
Lockwood, Primrose/Mills, Elaine
One Winter's Night
Luttrell, Ida/Giannini, Enzo
Milo's Toothache
Maestro, Betsy and Giulio
Ferryboat

McDermott, Gerald
Raven
Milton,Joyce/Roe, Richard
Dinosaur Days
Milton, Joyce/Langford, Alton
Whales the Gentle Giants
Novak, Matt
Mr. Floop's Lunch
Paul, Jan S./Linden, Madelaine Gill
Hortense
Pedersen, Judy
Out in the Country
Pilkey, Dav
Dragon Gets By
Pilkey, Dav
Dragon's Merry Christmas
Porte, Barbara Ann/Abolafia, Yossi
Harry Gets An Uncle
Pizer, Abigail
Nosey Gilbert
Potter, Beatrix/McPhail, David
The Tale of Peter Rabbit
Rylant, Cynthia/Stevenson, Sucie
Henry And Mudge Take The Big Test
Ryland, Cynthia/Stevenson, Sucie
Henry And Mudge And The Long Weekend
Ryland, Cynthia/Stevenson, Sucie
Henry And Mudge And The Wild Wind
Sandlin, Joan
The Long Way to a New Land
Say, Allen
A River Dream
Smath, Jerry
Pretze And Pop's Closetful Of Stories
Standiford, Natalie/Cook, Donald
The Bravest Dog Ever
Testa, Fulvio
If You Look Around
Tompert, Ann/Hoffman, Rosekrans
Sue Patch and the Crazy Clocks

Turner, Charles/Mathis, Melissa Bay
The Turtle And The Moon
Ward, Lynd
The Biggest Bear
Wildsmith, Brian
Pelican
Wood, Audrey
Tugford Wanted to be Bad
Ziefert, Harriet/Smith, Mavis
Bob And Shirley - A Tale Of
Two Lobsters
Ziefert, Harriet/Mandel, Suzy
Under the Water

Guiding Discussion With Young Children
Suggestions for Parents

The warmth and pleasure we feel as we read special stories to children is continued as we then share points of view, insights and experiences afterward. We dare not let the chance for good talk escape by ignoring the questions our children pose.

As we know, children follow specific steps in learning how to read, but equally important in developing a love of reading is the way we handle conversation about what was read. Adult-child interaction and discussion are very important from the first "point and name" books when we ask, "Where's the banana?" "Can you touch the shoes?", to more detailed pictures when asking, "What's on the man's head?", or "What's the baby eating?" Young children react with excitement and position themselves close by in anticipation of the first words of favorite stories and later ask their own questions, "What's that?" or ". .he doing?"

As we go on to stories with more complicated plots, young children still stop us along the way with questions and comments. These may relate to the actual story or be drawn from the youngster's views of an ever-expanding world. By pausing to respond to these questions, we show that we value the child's reactions and "doors" open, leading to new growth and learning. By not correcting the child's responses or imposing our own reactions, we can build an atmosphere of trust. It is critical at this stage to show respect for the child's remarks, as a critical or corrective comment or even a negative reaction signals disapproval and the idea that the adult has all the answers and the child's job is to guess them. Even responses that appear way "off base" to us may make sense to the child. Simple comments like, "That's interesting" or "I hadn't thought of that," go a long way toward prompting creative thinking. We continue to share questions, open-ended ones, ones with no right or wrong answers, questions of wonderment. We continue to encourage all responses especially those which show emotional involvement with the story.

While not all responses are overtly detectable, many can be seen on the child's face and in his body language. A sober expression, a grin and a chuckle are signs. So are looks of interest, enjoyment and sadness. Sometimes feelings are spoken aloud or statements made about liking and disliking a character, or what the child would do as a character. Relating personal experiences from his or her own life or expressing pleasure at hearing another story by the same author also show involvement.

For the very young child, a fine way to encourage active response is by using wordless books. These are the true picture books — the pictures provide the entire plot and give the pre-reader the opportunity to tell the story himself. Usually, this telling will be a description of the action. If the child adds inferences, elaborations or emotions (of the characters or his own) all the better. The parent has a chance to add details afterward, especially if the child asks you to tell the story after he or she has told it. This model may well carry over to the next story without words.

As vocabulary and verbal skills expand, discussion possibilities are unlimited. The child may ask a question about something not understood or want to express feelings, fears, angers or doubts which have surfaced as a result of a particularly moving story. There may be a desire to retell the story to you or someone else, now or at a later time.

The tale may be changed, shortened, updated or reinvented according to the child's desires. Because this kind of interaction starts with the child, it needs to be treated with respect and patience. As an adult, you can start conversation with personal thoughts and reactions of your own. A particular illustration, use of description, special part of the story or memory from your childhood could trigger comments to share. You might want to relate the story to something known to the youngster or use it to anticipate and set up a similar experience. This special bonding of child to parent that results from reading and talking together is of great value for building and strengthening life-long communication.

Children from homes where reading is emphasized, and an active involvement with their world encouraged, come to discussions with a tremendous amount of mental resources. By this we mean ideas and remembered emotions. These are drawn from the child's life experiences as well as his reading experiences. These combine to become, what we call, the "experience file." Components of this experience file are stored in the brain waiting to be called upon for use in formal or informal discussion sessions or in active application to real life situations. The brain is like a computer receiving information and storing it on a disk to be retrieved later. As an example: first grader Victoria remembered that it bothered her to read about alligators capturing other animals for food and how she didn't like to see the prey dangling from their mouths. She also remembered that the alligator's nose and mouth were different from the crocodile's and after her first grade teacher presented a lesson on reptiles, Victoria was able to offer this information to the class. Reading the book about crocodiles and alligators gave her facts about reptiles that were stored in her file and since she had been emotionally involved during the reading (saddened by the dead prey), the facts had a lasting effect. The reptile discussion sparked recall of information and since the contribution to the discussion was praised by the teacher, Victoria's self esteem was raised and the good feeling caused her to want to read and retrieve again.

Your child already has an expanding experience file, and just as help was needed in learning to tie shoes, ride a bike or recite the alphabet, so is guidance and practice needed to demonstrate how to recall and use information from that file to make sense out of the world around him or her.

In looking at the foundations of personality development, child study experts emphasize the importance of building many experiences, observations and attitudes into the child's emerging self thus encouraging reflection, comparison and analysis. This ever-growing "data base" can be called upon in making decisions and moral judgements, assessing situations or taking actions. Discussions that grow out of sharing literature provide modeling for the process. Providing reading experiences for children and then creating opportunities for thoughtful sharing afterward will help make important contributions to their personal growth and maturity.

A Guide to Initiating Conversational, High-level Discussion

From the basic questions we asked our baby, "Where's your bottle?", to a toddler conversation about why the oatmeal was too hot to eat, to the preschooler questioning the value of being truthful and telling you what he would do, we see a fairly predictable progression of questioning emerging in our children. As parents and teachers, we take cues from our children and initiate conversations that challenge their thinking. By answering their questions, responding and posing questions of our own, children are very naturally drawn into conversation. Curious to know more, or sparked by an adult's response, the child reaches for a favorite book or encyclopedia for more learning. We recognize the importance of our talk.

As children emerge from their preschool years and enter school, they display a wide range of expressive language skills. Some children are very verbal, willing to share stories about everything with everyone while others are more reserved, preferring to have conversation with another person - only wanting to speak when asked a question. It is the teacher's job to teach to both extremes and to the wide range of verbal skills of students in between. It is clear that children have academic advantages when they are placed in learning environments with adults who value thinking, use mind--challenging questions and are willing to model the strategies of high-level discussion. With practice, their students grow, become comfortable with open-ended questions and begin to use information and facts they have acquired to support their ideas and opinions clearly and concisely in discussion. Able to solve problems and think creatively, these children are prepared to meet the challenges of a technological society.

We offer the following outline of prompts that we used in our teaching and hope you will enjoy the process of "making up" your own questions to ponder with your children. While it is important to ask some basic questions to ascertain clarity of a story, we do not want discussion to stop here.

In order to make the act of posing questions a natural and comfortable process, you need to have a clear idea of what is meant by "open-ended" questions (questions with no right or wrong answers). A good way to do that is by learning to create questions yourself and then taking a few minutes to discuss possible answers with another adult. (Keep in mind that the questions in the "Prompt For Fiction-Analysis" section are for your use and are ones you will ask yourself **not** the child.)

PROCEDURE:
1. Read the book or story silently to yourself.
2. Work through the questions in the "Prompts For Fiction-Analysis" and check those especially appropriate for what you have read.
3. Turn your answer into an open-ended question. Here are some phrases and examples to get you started, using *Hansel and Gretel* as an example. **What other ways** might Hansel and Gretel's father have used to solve the problems other than abandoning the children? **What could have happened** if the bird had led Hansel and Gretel out of the forest? **Suppose** the witch had been a good witch - **how could the story have changed?** If you had been abandoned in the forest, what would you say or do? How is *Hansel and Gretel* like *Little Red Riding Hood?* (the stories need not be obviously similar)

EXAMPLE:
1. Read *Hansel and Gretel* to yourself.
2. Check II (Characters), C (Problems), Question 1.
3. You feel that many of the characters have problems.
   a. The father is torn, in loyalty, between his children and his wife.

b. The stepmother does not want the children to continue to live with them.
c. The witch is cruel and abusive.
d. The children feel unloved.

You decide that you want to focus on the stepmother and her problem(s). Your answer to the questions, "Does this character have a problem?" and "How does he/she plan to solve it?" is: The stepmother lives with children she resents and wants to be rid of them, so she makes plans to abandon them in the forest."

4. You formulate an open-ended question from this answer. Why did the stepmother choose this way to rid herself of the children?
    Possible responses from a child:
    a. Killing them would be too violent and there couldn't be a happy ending.
    b. She could tell other people the children ran away - they wouldn't blame her.
    c. Maybe deep down she wanted to give them a chance to survive.
    Some other possible directions this discussion may follow could be:
    a. If you had been Hansel and Gretel, would you rather stay in the home or risk the dangers of the forest?
    b. What would have happened if the father had not gone along with the plan?

PROMPTS FOR FICTION - ANALYSIS

I. **The Story**
    A. Basic information
        1. What is the significance of the title? What does it mean and add to the story?
        2. Is there realism or fantasy in the story or even a combination?
        3. What moods and emotions do you experience as the story progresses?

B. What happens
1. How did the situation get to be that way?
2. What does the text tell me?
3. What do the illustrations tell me?
4. Are there points in the story where a predictive question would be significant? (What do you think is going to happen now? Now what could he/she do?)
C. Comparisons
1. What other stories have I read that talked about the same or similar subjects?
2. What other stories evoked similar feelings and emotions?
D. Changes
1. Is there a change in the environment or a natural phenomenon? (Day to night, seasons, gathering rain clouds to rainbow, birth and growth of animals, etc.?)
2. Is there a change in a character's social situation or status? (pauper to prince)
3. Does the character learn to realize something?
4. How would things have been different if one element of the story had been changed?

II. **Characters**
A. Basic Information
1. What do I know about a character?
2. What can I learn about the character from the other characters?
3. What are the relationships among the characters?
4. What clues does the story give about a character's morals and values?
5. How did the character change in the course of the story? What caused the change(s)?
B. Behavior
1. Why did the character do what she/he did?
2. Was the behavior justified?
3. Did he/she learn anything?
4. How would I have acted (felt) in the same circumstances?

     5. How would I act the next time?

     6. What did you like about a particular character? Dislike?

     7. Did the behavior go along with values that were stated?

C. Problem(s)

     1. Does the character have a problem? How does he/she solve it?

     2. What are some other ways the problem could have been solved? Could it have been avoided? How?

     3. Is there a similar problem in other stories I have read? How did hose characters solve it?

     4. How would I have solved the problem?

D. Comparison(s)

     1. How is this character like/unlike other characters or persons I know?

     2. Is there anything about this character that is present in myself or my child?

     3. How can depth or intensity of character traits be rated? Between characters, who is more evil or most compassionate?

E. Role(s)

     1. Why did the author include each character? How would the story be different if anyone had been left out?

     2. Did any minor character turn out to be important later in the story?

     3. What was the "job" of each character? (Hero, heroine, narrator?)

III. **The craft of the author/illustrator**

A. Special techniques: author

     1. What words did the author use to create especially vivid pictures?

     2. How did the author get me to feel an emotion?

     3. How did the author make the characters believable?

     4. What clues did the author give about how the story could turn out?

     5. Why did the author choose to say something as he/she did?

B. Special techniques: illustrator
1. Are the artist's media, style and moods in harmony with the author's words?
2. Did the pictures help me place myself in the time and setting of the story?
3. What did I get from the artwork that was not written in the text?
4. Is there a continuing detail that appears frequently or on every page? What is its significance?
C. Comparison(s)
1. By looking at two or more books by the same author or illustrator, can I see a definite style? What unique characteristics are there?
2. Do I know of any other authors or illustrators whose style is similar?
3. In comparing at least two books about the same story (especially fairy tales) but with different authors or illustrators, how are they alike or different? Which would be my preference and why?

Conclusion

Raising children has to be the most exhausting, frustrating, joyous, confusing, exhilarating job we encounter in our lives. I will never forget the anxieties of bringing our first baby home, the all night terror of high temperatures, the apprehension of parent/teacher conferences, and the pain of helping my child work through rejection. But, those times seem very long ago on most days and just like yesterday when our grandchildren come for the day.

I am knee deep in grandchildren on the days their mother works, reminded, once again, of the energy it takes to keep a family going. Sibling rivalry is back, the "ouchies", the tantrums, the thumps and bumps, the potty problems, forts made from sofa cushions, peanut butter, giggles, smooches and hugs remind me that kids haven't changed one bit.

A significant change I do see is that children today require a stronger commitment from those who love them because there are too many choices and so many distractions. There is confusion as to what is best for our children. Understanding the emotional and intellectual needs of children, keeps parents focused on their role as the first and most important teacher and nurturer.

Especially critical for parents and those adults caring for young children is the challenge of providing stimulating activities. A book in a diaper bag to entertain a restless baby, a shared moment of watching a spider spin a web, designing and building a space craft from Legos, paper and paint, music, puzzles and clay, are activities which spark interests. Back yards can be converted to nature centers, expanding the child's world. We never know how and when these experiences will be "called up" and used, but children who have a wide base of information have more to talk and write about. By using our creativity and resources from our community, we are able to provide interesting days for our children.

If we have introduced you to a new book, author or illustrator, provided encouragement and support in finding those special books for your child, aided you in the understanding of the process of becoming a reader, then our reward will be knowing that children everywhere will have a greater chance for becoming readers because they will have caring adults close by sharing the joy of glorious books.

ORDERING INFORMATION

Read to Me. . . And I'll Read to You — **$12.95**

book of titles, lists and background information - featuring:

- Discussion of the **five** kinds of books **before** story books.
- Suggestions for initiating conversation with young children which promote thinking.
- Integration of books with the stages of development of children from birth through third grade.
- 640+ books for children to read, arranged by 8 levels of difficulty - Begins with books of very little text and many picture clues, and steadily progresses through each level. The books are readily available in libraries and bookstores.
- 1660+ books for **reading aloud**, arranged by age level - This list includes the finest children's books by outstanding authors and illustrators.

Out of the Classroom. . . Into the Home — **$9.95**

20 minute audio tape

This recording of warm, specific dialogue between a parent and teacher addresses the most frequently asked questions about reading and explains to parents how they can:

- improve reading progress tremendously by providing daily shared practice
- enhance their child's understanding by promoting conversation/discussion
- help children make easier, meaningful connections between old information and new
- model their own thinking, helping with problem solving and reasoning
- keep children's curiosity and motivation for learning to read strong
- provide incentives for reluctant readers
- find books children love by looking for those which involve their emotions
- encourage problem solving and reasoning by modeling their own thinking strategies

Navy fabric child-sized tote bag **imprinted with the message— $5.95**

Impact-School and Home-Together-Our Children, Our Priority

On the Wings of Books — *$34.95*

50 minute video tape with book, *Read to Me. . . And I'll Read to You*

Included in this "How-To" video for parents with infants through third grade, are answers to these questions:

- How can I give my child the lifelong love of reading?
- What books are appropriate for reading to my infant, toddler, preschooler, and school-age child and why?
- How do I encourage book talk with discussion other than traditional factual questions?
- How does the "experience file" affect the achievement of my child?
- How does discussion of art media and techniques in children's books enhance art appreciation?

ORDER FORM

Read to me ...
And I'll read to you

Date_____

Name_____

Address_____

City_____State_____Zip_____

Please send me the following items and quantities indicated:

_____ copies of the book - ***Read to Me. . . And I'll Read to You*** @ $12.95 each.
_____ copies of the audio tape - ***Out of the Classroom. . . Into the Home*** @ $9.95 each.
_____ tote bag - ***Navy fabric child-size tote bag*** @ $5.95 each.
_____ tote bag - Black canvas imprinted ***Read Aloud Tote*** @ $9.95 each.
_____ copies of the video & book - ***On the Wings of Books*** @ $34.95 each.

I have enclosed _____ for the items above plus an additional _____for shipping and handling.

TOTAL AMOUNT ENCLOSED_____

ADD POSTAGE AND HANDLING FOR ORDERS TOTALING:	
up to $12.95	$3.95
$12.96 to $25.00	$4.95
$25.01 to $50.00	$5.95
$50.01 to $75.00	$7.95
$75.01 or more	$9.50
Ohio Residents Add 6% for Sales Tax	

SEND ORDERS TO:

The Cleary Connection
P.O. Box 310
Arcanum, Ohio 45304